Reptiles & Amphibians
of the Eastern Caribbean

Anita Malhotra and Roger S. Thorpe

School of Biological Sciences,
University of Wales, Bangor, UK

CARIBBEAN

First published 1999 by
MACMILLAN EDUCATION LTD
London and Oxford
Companies and representatives throughout the world

ISBN 0-333-69141-5

2011 2010 2009 2008 2007 2006
13 12 11 10 9 8 7 6 5 4 3 2

This book is printed on paper suitable for recycling and
made from fully managed and sustained forest sources.

Typeset by 𝙏 Tek-Art, Croydon, Surrey
Colour separation by Tenon & Polert Colour Scanning Ltd
Printed in Thailand

A catalogue record for this book is available from the
British Library.

Illustration by Martin Sanders

Front cover photograph: Whistling frog, *Eleutherodactylus martinicensis*
(Trois Rivières, Guadeloupe). Courtesy A. Malhotra

Back cover photograph: Male Dominican anole, *Anolis oculatus*, feeding
on a cockroach. Courtesy A. Malhotra

Contents

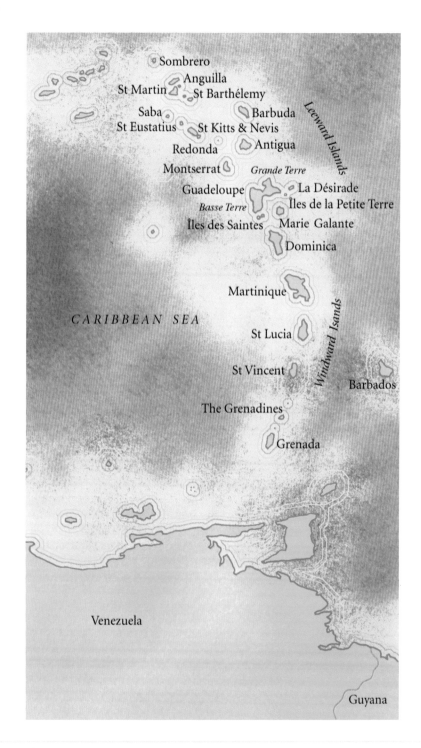

Sombrero

Anguilla

St Martin · St Barthélemy

Saba · Barbuda

St Eustatius · St Kitts & Nevis

Redonda · Antigua

Montserrat · *Grande Terre*

Guadeloupe · La Désirade

Basse Terre · Îles de la Petite Terre

Îles des Saintes · Marie Galante

Dominica

Leeward Islands

Martinique

CARIBBEAN SEA

St Lucia

St Vincent

Windward Islands

Barbados

The Grenadines

Grenada

Venezuela

Guyana

Preface

This book is intended primarily as a field guide to the approximately one hundred species of reptiles and amphibians that occur on the islands of the Eastern Caribbean, which stretch from Sombrero in the north to Grenada in the south. Our knowledge of the reptiles and amphibians of the Eastern Caribbean has been built up over the last 12 years of research on their evolutionary ecology, particularly in Dominica. As well as serving as an introduction to the biology of these often-maligned animals for those who have not previously been interested in them, we hope that this book will also appeal to amateur and professional herpetologists. We have tried to incorporate results from the latest research (including our own) into our accounts.

The book begins with an introduction to the historical and ecological background of the islands of the Eastern Caribbean, and to the biology of reptiles and amphibians and their cultural and ecological significance. The next chapter introduces the main groups (families and genera) of reptiles and amphibians present in the Eastern Caribbean, including a general description of their biology, their worldwide distribution and significance as well as their representation in the Lesser Antilles. This chapter will contain information that is common to all species and will not be repeated in individual species accounts. The islands often have a very similar reptile and amphibian community structure, even if the exact species present are different. Consequently, we have then focused on a single island community in particular and describe it in some detail. We have chosen Dominica, not only because we are most familiar with it, but also (unlike many other islands) the community is virtually intact, having escaped the extinctions experienced on other islands as a result of human activities (e.g. habitat destruction or introductions of foreign predators). We then move on to present a series of island profiles, in which the specific features and species of each island are described in detail.

The glossary explains any technical terms that may not be familiar to the non-specialist. A checklist of species on each island is included for easy reference, allowing both the range of any given species or the species present on any island to be seen at a glance. The references list sources wherever possible, and will provide a starting point for further reading for those interested in finding out more.

We would like to thank the staff of the Forestry and Wildlife Department of the Commonwealth of Dominica, in particular Arlington James who always displayed enthusiastic interest in our work. We also thank the Forestry Department of St Lucia (particularly Christopher Cox, Donald Anthony and Lyndon John) and the Forestry Division of Antigua and Barbuda (particularly McRonnie Henry and Everett Williams). Jenny Daltry (of Flora and Fauna International) provided useful information about islands that we have not personally visited. Many people – too many to name individually – have helped in a variety of ways during our work on these islands, and we would like to thank all of them for their warmth and hospitality. Roger Thorpe would particularly like to thank his postgraduate students (Mark Day, Anita Malhotra, Nick Giannasi, James Reardon, Alex Jones and Andy Stenson and assorted MSc ecologists) for their fellowship.

Finally, changes in nomenclature and information regarding distributions inevitably introduce errors into this type of book. The authors will be grateful for any pertinent information so that they can incorporate it into later editions.

Dr A. Malhotra and Professor R. S. Thorpe
School of Biological Sciences
University of Wales Bangor
Gwynedd LL57 2UW
UK

Acknowledgements

The authors and publishers wish to acknowledge, with thanks, the following photographic sources for which copyright remains with the photographers:

John Cancalosi: Plates 54, 57, 58
David Corke: Plates 75, 76, 79, 80, 83
Alex Jones: Plates 42, 69, 70, 86 87
Hinrich Kaiser: Plates 81, 88
Anita Malhotra: Plates 4, 5, 8–11, 14–16, 21, 22, 28, 29, 31, 32, 35, 38, 39, 41, 43, 44, 47, 49, 50, 52, 55, 56, 59–63, 66–68, 90, 91
Roger S. Thorpe: Plates 1–3, 6, 7, 12, 13, 17–20, 23–27, 30, 33, 34, 36, 37, 40, 45, 46, 48, 51, 53, 64, 65, 71–74, 77, 78, 82, 84, 85, 89

Introduction

THE ISLANDS OF THE EASTERN CARIBBEAN

This book covers the islands of the Eastern Caribbean (or Lesser Antilles) from Sombrero in the north to Grenada in the south. This is not an arbitrary choice, as a common geological origin and faunal similarity unites these islands. They are all volcanic islands (with the exception of Barbados, see below), which have formed at the eastern edge of the block of the earth's crust known as the Caribbean Plate. As the western edge of the Atlantic Plate pushes under this (i.e. subducts), it melts and is forced up to the surface once again as molten lava. There have been several episodes of volcanism along this subduction zone. The older islands (which stretch from Sombrero in the north to St Lucia in the south) resulted from an episode that occurred around 23 million years ago (mya). These later underwent a period of submergence under the sea, during which the volcanic rock was eroded and capped with limestone. Later, around 5–10 mya, a new period of volcanism caused the eruption of a new chain of islands to the west of the earlier chain, stretching almost the entire length of the Eastern Caribbean from Saba in the north to Grenada in the south. These young islands are still active (e.g. the volcano in Montserrat has been erupting since 1995, after a long period of dormancy). The island of Barbados has a unique origin among the Lesser Antillean islands. Rather than being volcanic, it consists of a part of ocean sediment that has been squeezed up to the surface by the Atlantic Plate as it slides under the Caribbean Plate[1]. To the north of the Lesser Antilles runs a deep-water channel called the Anegada Passage, which forms a natural break between them and the islands of the Puerto Rican bank. To the south, there is another deep-water channel (the Trinidad–Grenada Passage) which separates them from Trinidad and Tobago, which are continental rather than oceanic islands and faunistically and geologically part of the South American mainland. Since the Lesser Antilles have never been connected to the mainland, their reptiles and amphibians have colonised by crossing over the sea, and have done so both northwards from South America and southwards from the Greater Antilles.

The younger islands of the Eastern Caribbean have tall mountain peaks which trap the moisture contained in the easterly Trade Winds blowing westwards from the Atlantic, and hence have high rainfall and lush vegetation. Since the wind blows roughly from the same direction (east to north-east) throughout the year, those islands in which the central spine of mountains form a continuous barrier have well-differentiated east and west coastal vegetation types, e.g. Basse Terre (the western island of Guadeloupe) and Dominica. The mountain peaks of these islands are also high enough to have distinct montane habitats, which provide the opportunity for the evolution of specialised endemic species. Smaller islands, or those which lack a continuous central mountain range, lack a distinct rain shadow (e.g. Montserrat). The older islands tend to be rather uniformly flat and arid, although erosion of the porous limestone may create some relief (e.g. the Grand Fonds area of Grande Terre, Guadeloupe).

BIOLOGY OF REPTILES AND AMPHIBIANS

Reptiles and amphibians are ectotherms (often misleadingly called cold-blooded) and therefore are dependent on obtaining energy directly from the sun. This may involve frequent sunbathing or basking for some fast-moving species that operate at high body temperatures (i.e. heliothermic). These species are usually active only during the day but others may be nocturnal (such as boa constrictors and frogs), crepuscular (i.e. mainly active at dusk and dawn, e.g. racers), or live in habitats where direct sunlight is not available (e.g. deep forest anoles). The latter do not bask and may operate over a wide range of (including fairly low) body temperatures. Since none of them use their own energy to maintain a body temperature higher than the surrounding environment (as mammals and birds do) they can survive on very low food intake. This allows reptilian predators to have relatively high predator–prey ratios. Most reptiles and amphibians are carnivores, but some regularly also take vegetable and fruit material (omnivores) while a few are largely vegetarian (e.g. tortoises and iguanas).

Most reptiles and amphibians in the Lesser Antilles do not have as distinct a breeding season as those from temperate regions. This is because of the warm temperatures and high rainfall throughout the year, making conditions suitable for reproduction at most times. There is, however, a peak of breeding which may occur at different times in species living in different habitats, and usually occurs at the end of the dry season. Most frogs, unlike their temperate relatives, are terrestrial and do not return to the water to breed. Instead, they have evolved a variety of adaptations to protect their shell-less eggs from drying out, such as utilising water that collects in leaf axils to lay their eggs, or making foam nests in which the eggs are laid and develop into adults without passing through an independent larval stage. Some lizards are parthenogenetic (they can reproduce without mating) and males are rare or non-existent. This makes them very good colonisers of new islands. Reptile eggs may be hard-shelled (e.g. geckos) or soft-shelled. The former can survive dry conditions but the latter are usually deposited in moist sand, earth or vegetation. Some species even retain the eggs within their bodies and give birth to live young (e.g. vipers).

Not many reptiles have a voice, one notable exception being the geckos. However, frogs are extremely vocal, the males use their voices to advertise themselves to other males (to warn them off) and females (to invite them to mate). The sound is produced by vocal chords and amplified by air-filled vocal sacs. Frogs tend to have species-specific calls, even though in most of the Lesser Antilles they do not coexist with similar species. Their calls may be adapted to their environment; e.g. the whistling frog, *Eleutherodactylus barlagnei,* from the highlands of Guadeloupe lives in moss mats in streams and has a high pitched whistle that pierces the sound of the flowing water.

Various defence strategies are used to defend themselves against natural enemies (e.g. birds, mammals and other reptiles). These include autotomy, in which lizards can voluntarily break off their tails. The muscles in the autotomised tail contract, producing whip-like movements, which distract the would-be predator and allow its owner time to make its escape. Only two of the Lesser Antilles have any venomous snakes (St Lucia and Martinique), both belonging to the South American genus of pit vipers, *Bothrops*. Their bite can be fatal but they are rarely seen (although reportedly extremely abundant on these islands). Some frogs and snakes exude noxious or unpleasant secretions when alarmed and these can be toxic in the former (e.g. the marine toad, *Bufo marinus*). Others simply rely on staying still and avoiding being seen (crypsis).

Reptiles and amphibians are generally easy to see, and some in fact are difficult to avoid noticing. Some, such as geckos and some anoles, are happy living alongside man in houses and gardens. The piercing whistles of the *Eleutherodactylus* frogs are a feature of the Eastern Caribbean nights and cannot be overlooked (although they are much more difficult to see than hear as they usually call from concealed perches). Some, e.g. iguanas and the giant frog known as the 'mountain chicken', may even be eaten, and others are used in traditional medicine, e.g. in Dominica, snake fat extracted from boas may be used to treat arthritis and a soup made from *Anolis* lizards is said to be good for asthmatics. However, other reptiles are secretive and escape notice even when they are widespread and abundant. Yet others may be restricted to small areas – either naturally or through elimination from the greater part of their former range (see Conservation).

To see reptiles and amphibians, it is important to know the species habitat and activity patterns, e.g. some species may be much more active and easy to see at dusk. Other species may be found by looking in suitable hiding places, e.g. in crevices of trees or under logs and rocks (but remember to replace the latter in their original positions). Frogs are, unsurprisingly, best found at night by following their calls, although they can be very hard to pinpoint. Any reptile or amphibian is best seen by moving slowly and quietly through suitable habitat, and many can be approached to quite a close distance, while a pair of close-focusing binoculars are useful for watching the larger, more wary species.

Lastly, it should be emphasised that there is seldom any justification for handling or harming any species. It is much more rewarding and interesting to observe and photograph an animal in its natural habitat while it is carrying out its natural behaviour. This is especially true of the two venomous snakes. Although potentially dangerous, snakes bite man primarily in defence, so if care is taken when walking through rough ground where these species occur and no attempt is made to interfere with the animal if encountered, then there is usually no danger. If a bite should occur, the victim should be treated for shock and transferred to a medical facility immediately, while observing for signs of envenomation (e.g. swelling at the site of the bite). On no account should the bite site be cut or sucked, or have any substance put on it, or a tourniquet applied as these 'treatments' often cause more damage than the bite itself. This advice is relevant to the species present in the Lesser Antilles and may not be more widely applicable.

A NOTE ON TAXONOMY

Most people are familiar with the concept of species. These are described by scientists by using a binomial Latin name which is conventionally written in italic script, the first word (written with a capital letter) representing the genus (a group of closely related species) and the second word being a unique species name. However, species may not be uniform in appearance. There may in fact be variation of several types present. First, within-population variation may result from growth (i.e. juveniles often look different from adults) or sexual differences (i.e. adult males and females look different). Individual variation may be present, either as continuous variation or polymorphism (taking two or more distinct forms). The latter may be mistaken for different species. Second, there may be between-population variation, which has a geographic pattern. This is often treated by naming subspecies (regional types), in which a third Latin name is added to the species name (i.e. it becomes a trinomial). This is intended to reflect the presence of some degree of reproductive isolation between these types, but which has not yet been completely established. In the Lesser Antilles, species which occur on more than one island are often given a separate subspecific name for each island, but there are also species which show considerable geographic variation within each island and these have also been split into separate subspecies. In some cases, the variation that has been recognised by subspecies designation is more likely to be the result of local adaptation to a variable environment (e.g. rain forest vs. xeric woodland), rather than a reflection of reproductive barriers between the populations. Even in cases where the variation does appear to be the result of more significant, genetically entrenched, differences between populations, the subspecies frequently fail to reflect the actual pattern of genetic differences. They can therefore be very misleading about the actual pattern of variation. We have not used subspecific designations in this book (although we do indicate if subspecies have been described) unless they have been supported by detailed morphological and/or genetic studies.

HOW TO USE THIS BOOK

This book is primarily a photographic guide. This will work well in the Lesser Antilles, as there are often only one or two species of any group on a single island. These groups (and many individual species) can be easily identified by means of photographs, and if you know which island you are on the most difficult part of the job is already done. In some instances, such as where there are two or more species of whistling frogs (*Eleutherodactylus*) present, it will not be possible to distinguish species from the photograph alone. However, even professional herpetologists using a proper scientific key may have difficulty in distinguishing these species. In these cases, we have tried to present as much information on distinguishing characteristics, distribution, habitat and behaviour as is available, or at the very least to point out that they may be confused. Readers should also bear in mind that any species may be illustrated by a single photograph, whereas there may in fact be considerable variation between islands, habitats, sexes and between adults and young of the same species. Where this is the case, this will also be highlighted in the text.

The scientific and common English name (where it exists) is given for each species. Vernacular names vary considerably from island to island, so they are not included. Superscripted numbers refer to the citations of the key literature listed in the References. Plate numbers are indicated in bold type. Descriptions of species with which we are not personally familiar were drawn largely from the invaluable reference by Schwartz and Henderson[2]. Reptiles and amphibians of the Lesser Antilles vary from some of the smallest (only a few centimetres long, e.g. dwarf geckos) to some of the largest (more than a few metres long, e.g. boa constrictors). The size of reptiles and amphibians is usually given as 'snout to vent length' (SVL) (i.e. excluding the tail) and this convention is followed in this book. For turtles and tortoises the length is that of the upper shell (carapace), given as a straight-line measurement. Most sizes are derived from the largest preserved specimens in museum collections, so occasionally larger specimens may be encountered in the field. All measurements are in metres (m), centimetres (cm) or millimetres (mm) (1 inch = 2.54 cm). In some species, such as the common iguana, the tail is very long so that the overall size of the animal may be over twice as long as suggested by the SVL.

Major Groups of Reptiles and Amphibians in the Eastern Caribbean

AMPHIBIANS

There are three living orders of amphibian, with about 4000 species worldwide: the apodans (caecelians), urodeles (newts and sala-manders) and anurans (frogs and toads). All amphibians have moist, bare skin and produce shell-less eggs and are therefore dependent upon water to some degree for reproduction. Being mainly insectivorous they are important in ecosystems and, because of their permeable skins, are particularly susceptible to environ-mental pollution. They may be used therefore as indicators of envi-ronmental quality. The Eastern Caribbean islands, being oceanic, have rather few amphibians, with only four families of anurans being represented. Of these, only 10 species (from two families) occur naturally. However, they include some of the largest amphib-ians (the introduced marine toad) as well as some of the smallest (whistling frogs of the genus *Eleutherodactylus*). The most wide-spread and numerous species belong to the family Leptodactylidae.

Family Leptodactylidae

This family is restricted to South and Central America, and has two widespread, naturally occurring, genera in the Eastern Caribbean. These are *Eleutherodactylus* (whistling frogs) and *Leptodactylus* (which includes the 'mountain chicken', an edible species). The for-mer genus contains a very large number of species, but only seven of these occur in the Lesser Antilles[3], while the latter genus is less diverse with just two species represented. They are wide-mouthed frogs with broad bodies. They mostly lay terrestrial eggs but otherwise show a diverse range of reproductive modes. Most *Eleutherodactlyus* are small in size (less than 60 mm SVL) and resemble tree frogs, as they are usually arboreal. Species of this genus are difficult to identify because the species are very similar to each other, and there may be a high degree of within-species variability in colour pattern. *Leptodactylus,* on the other hand, can reach large sizes (up to 167 mm SVL) and are usually ground-living.

Family Dendrobatidae

This family of terrestrial or partly arboreal, often brightly coloured, frogs includes the infamous poison-arrow frogs (so named because of the potent skin toxins possessed by some members of the family, which are used by certain South American tribes to coat arrow tips with toxic substances). They are small, slim frogs with slender limbs with the toe and fingertips characteristically expanded into small adhesive discs. Until recently they were thought to be restricted to the mainland of South and Central America but a new species was recently discovered from the highlands of Martinique[4]. Not much is known about its habits, but other species of the genus *Colostethus* are known to have complex social behaviour. Either, or both, sexes may be territorial and they defend their territories against other frogs with displays that may include calling, colour change, posturing and finally chases, attacks and wrestling. Only a few eggs are laid on land and tadpoles may be transported to water on the backs of the adults.

Family Hylidae

Members of this family are known as 'true tree frogs'. It is a very large family, with a widespread distribution in the eastern and western hemispheres. Their body form is flattened and slender, with smooth skins, long legs and (often) webbed feet, and in most species the tips of the fingers and toes are enlarged into circular discs with claw-like terminal structures. As their name suggests, they spend most of their time in the trees where they capture flying insects, only rarely coming to the ground. Despite their widespread occurrence, the presence of a single species of this family in the Lesser Antilles is likely to be due to its introduction by man. Most (including the species represented here, *Scinax rubra*) lay large numbers of eggs in standing water, with the tadpoles hatching into free-swimming larvae.

Family Bufonidae

Only the marine toad, *Bufo marinus*, represents this cosmopolitan family (the true toads), in the Eastern Caribbean. It resembles other members of the family in being terrestrial (despite its name), and is short and stout with short legs and a rough, warty skin. In prominent glands just behind the head (the parotoid glands) it produces toxins which it can squirt a distance of up to 1 m, into the face of a potential predator. Eggs are laid in large numbers in water, where they hatch into free-swimming tadpoles. It has most probably been introduced from its native South, Central and North American range to control cane pests (as it has been in many other parts of the world), hence it is often also known as the cane toad.

REPTILES

Reptiles are characterised by having scaly skins that inhibit water loss; they lay shelled eggs, which allow them to live in xeric habitats. Despite their superficial similarity, reptiles are made up of diverse groups, which probably do not share a common ancestor. Amphisbaenians (worm lizards) are not represented in the Eastern Caribbean, and crocodiles (e.g. *Caiman crocodilus* **(1)**) may be present only as occasional vagrants from South America. Fourteen families belonging to two orders (the testudines, or turtles and tortoises, and the saurians, or lizards and snakes) are present.

1. Caiman, *Caiman crocodilus* (Surinam), are vagrants in the southern islands

Turtles, terrapins and tortoises

This ancient group of reptiles is characterised by possessing a bony shell that encloses the body, which may be covered by bony plates or tough skin. They may be terrestrial, semi-aquatic (in fresh or brackish water) or completely marine. Sea turtles cannot retract their heads into their shells, and have a streamlined body and fore-limbs modified into paddle-like flippers. Four species of marine turtles, three semi-aquatic terrapins and one terrestrial tortoise are found in the Lesser Antilles. The marine turtles are largely (but not entirely) pan-tropical and introductions have had a significant impact on the distribution of the other families. A very large number of species are considered endangered (see Conservation).

Families Chelonidae and Dermochelidae

Around the coast of Lesser Antillean islands, green (*Chelonia mydas*), leatherback (*Dermochelys coriacea*), loggerhead (*Caretta caretta*), and hawksbill (*Eretmochelys imbricata*) turtles can be seen. These turtles tend to be widespread throughout the Lesser Antilles (hence they are not listed under each island).

The leatherback turtle is the largest living turtle, and belongs to a family of its own. It has a grey-black or blue-black skin-covered carapace up to 180 cm long. The shell is reduced to bony remnants embedded within thick, oily, connective tissue, with characteristic and clearly defined longitudinal ridges. It can maintain its body temperature several degrees above that of the surrounding water, because of its large size. It is therefore capable of visiting colder waters than the other species of turtle. It feeds primarily on jelly-fish and is primarily a deep-sea animal, but like all sea turtles, females need to come ashore on to sandy beaches to excavate a hole to lay their eggs (clutches may exceed 100 eggs at a time, each being 5–6 cm in diameter).

The loggerhead turtle has a large bulbous head and a humped reddish brown carapace up to 110 cm long which is longer than wide and lacks a clearly defined central ridge. The plates have whitish edges. It is a carnivorous species, feeding on molluscs, fish, coelenterates and crabs when adult. Most nesting sites are in temperate regions, and are usually on continental margins rather than oceanic islands[5].

Hawksbill turtles **(2)** are the species most likely to be seen in the Lesser Antilles. As their name suggests, they have a pronounced

2. Hawksbill turtle, *Eretmochelys imbricata,* feeding at 35 m depth (Saba)

beak-like face. The carapace may reach just under a metre in length, with overlapping plates (which are marked with radiating lines), a clear median ridge and a serrated posterior margin. They are omnivorous with a tendency towards carnivory, feeding on benthic invertebrates such as molluscs, tunicates and sponges (including species that contain siliceous spicules and are known to produce toxins). It has been hunted for the outer scutes, which are used as 'tortoise-shell' (see Conservation). On the northern coast of South America it nests between May and December, with a peak between July and October. This species is hunted and eaten in the Eastern Caribbean, although apparently the meat of this species may be toxic in some populations.

The green turtle has a large, oval, greenish to dark brown carapace up to 140 cm long and, despite the lack of the characteristic features of hawksbills, it can sometimes be confused with them. However, the presence of one rather than two pairs of scales between the eyes (prefrontals) is a definitive distinguishing feature. The first-year young of green turtles are carnivorous but the adults are primarily herbivorous, feeding on seagrass in shallow coastal areas. It is heavily hunted for food in some parts of the world with a concomitant reduction in numbers (see Conservation) despite its prolific habits (in other parts of the world, they have been recorded laying 11 clutches of over 100 eggs each at approximately 10-day intervals).

Family Testudinidae

Tortoises are found in most tropical and subtropical parts of the world except Australia. They are all terrestrial and may be small to extremely large in size. They have stout and armoured limbs, with the forelimbs somewhat flattened. The genus *Geochelone*, which includes the Galapagos Giant Tortoise, is the only representative of this family to inhabit South America (it is also found in Africa, India and Southeast Asia). The sole species in the Lesser Antilles, *Geochelone carbonaria*, is reported from a number of Eastern Caribbean islands. This species is widespread in tropical South America and in other West Indian islands and it may have been introduced into the Lesser Antilles by Amerindians (possibly for food as it is reportedly good to eat) and/or more recently. In the Lesser Antilles it inhabits forest and grasslands where it eats carrion as well as its main diet of fruits, leaves and flowers. It is mainly active in the early morning and evening, resting in the heat of the day. Courtship has not been described in this species, but in its relatives it may be quite active, with the male chasing the female and butting and biting her. Copulation can be precarious, with the male often losing his balance and falling off the female. It involves thrusts accompanied by a 'clucking' call by the male. A few spherical brittle-shelled eggs are laid in an excavated hole and the young, around 40–50 mm long, emerge after 5 months.

Family Emydidae

All members of this family have been introduced into the Eastern Caribbean, and are restricted to a few localities on the French islands of Guadeloupe and Marie Galante. They are semi-aquatic and, unlike their terrestrial relatives, are mainly carnivorous or omnivorous, feeding on a variety of aquatic organisms as well as opportunistically on carrion. Eggs, unlike those of sea turtles, are elongated and may be leathery or brittle-shelled and are laid in small clutches.

Family Pelomedusidae

This family consists of African and South American side-necked turtles. The neck cannot be retracted into its shell, and instead is bent to one side. Only one species is present, which has been introduced from its native Africa. In their native habitat, these turtles occupy deeper, still waters and rivers, nesting on sandy riverbanks, often in huge aggregations. They scavenge fish and feed on fruit and fresh-water invertebrates.

◆ Lizards

Lizards of the Lesser Antilles are among the most familiar reptiles, many of them being abundant and obvious, active during the day and often living in close proximity to humans. Several families are present, two of which are restricted to the neotropics. Most lizards are carnivores, but a few (less than 2 per cent of all known species) are herbivorous. Most lizards have a range of social behaviour that includes colour changes, body inflation, push-ups, jaw gaping, tail waving and other species-specific signals.

Family Iguanidae

This includes the giant iguanas, which are among the largest living reptiles, as well as the smaller, ubiquitous anoles. There was originally also one species of the genus *Leiocephalus* (placed by some authors in a separate family, Tropiduridae) which was endemic to the island of Martinique and is now extinct.

The family is widely distributed in the New World, although a few representatives occur further afield in Fiji and Madagascar. All species of the family are diurnal, living on the ground as well as in trees. The green or common iguana, *Iguana iguana,* is familiar as a pet, and is found in the Lesser Antilles as well as in other Caribbean islands and South and Central America. However, its sister species, *Iguana delicatissima,* is endemic to the Lesser Antilles. It is smaller than the green iguana, and is endangered through much of its range (see Island Profiles and Conservation chapters). Large iguanas are mainly herbivores, and while they may not move very far from day to day, they are nevertheless capable of moving fast. They will often dive off their arboreal perches to crash to the ground through the branches when sufficiently alarmed, after which they make off at great speed. Iguanas may lay large clutches of eggs (up to 45 in green iguanas) in hollow trees or holes excavated in soft ground. Young iguanas are a beautiful apple-green colour. As they get older they usually become duller slate-grey, although some green iguanas may be dramatically coloured and banded with black as adults. The two species look very similar, but can be distinguished by the presence of a large circular plate below the tympanum and a distinctive banded tail in the common iguana. Although both species may be seen in aggregations (especially the younger animals), iguanas are territorial. They have a complex repertoire of social behaviour, including posturing, head bobbing and dewlap distension. They have a threat display which involves gaping and inflation to make themselves appear even bigger, but can also defend themselves by biting, scratching and using their tails as whips.

The second genus of iguanids present is *Anolis,* which contains the second largest number of species of any vertebrate genus in the world (after *Eleutherodactylus* frogs). There are over 150 species in the Caribbean alone. Because of this huge diversity, and their interesting and easily observed behaviour, they have been a focus for evolutionary and ecological research for many years. There are two groups of species present in the Lesser Antilles, the species in each being closely related to each other, but only distantly related to those in the other group. One group has invaded the islands from South America, moving northwards as far as Martinique, while the other group has invaded from the Greater Antilles and has moved southwards as far as Dominica. In the Lesser Antilles, there are never more than two species of anole naturally present, and many islands have only one species. The coexisting species must share the resources available in some way in order to continue coexisting, and they do this primarily by taking different sized prey. In anoles, jaw length is closely correlated to prey size, so on two-species islands the species are different in body size. In the southern group, they also divide up space so that one species occupies the more xeric coastal habitats and the other the more mesic highland interior of the island. Anoles have colourful throat fans or dewlaps (usually only males have these) which they use to signal to other males to defend their territories, or to females, to attract them to mate. This behaviour by males often exposes them to visually hunting predators. Females may also be territorial and fight with each other. As well as being (largely) colourful lizards, anoles also have the ability to change colour very quickly, and this ability has earned them the name 'American chameleons'. They use this to express emotion (a stressed anole goes dark very quickly) or possibly also to thermoregulate, as a dark animal will absorb energy from the sun more quickly. Anoles have toes that are specially adapted to their arboreal lifestyle, having gripping structures (see geckos). Anoles only ever lay a single egg at a time, although these may be laid at frequent intervals. The smaller species eat mainly insects and other invertebrates but may occasionally eat berries and other plant material.

Family Gekkonidae

Geckos are a diverse and widespread family of lizards, being found all over the tropical and subtropical areas of the world, frequently on oceanic islands. Most geckos are nocturnal and hunt mainly insects largely by sight, so that they have very large eyes. Unlike most other lizards, most geckos do not have 'eyelids' which they can close, but instead the eye is covered by a transparent 'spectacle'. They are frequently excellent climbers, and can scale the smoothest of surfaces with a combination of claws and adhesive toe pads. These toe pads consist of fine plate-like structures (lamellae) which are composed of large numbers of very fine, hair-like setae. These setae can provide contact with minute irregularities in the surface of the substrate. Also unlike other lizards, most geckos have a voice (although it can be very inconspicuous in some species) which is used in territorial defence and mating. Some geckos are frequently found in association with human habitations ('house geckos'), and have been distributed throughout the world by man (usually accidentally). The genus *Hemidactylus* is a typical example. Geckos may vary considerably in size, and in the Lesser Antilles are represented by some of the smallest as well as some of the largest. They typically lay one or two eggs with brittle calcareous shells, often laying them in communal sites.

The genus *Sphaerodactylus* (dwarf geckos) is only found in the Caribbean and surrounding areas of the mainland. They are among the smallest lizards in the world, with adults being no larger than 40 mm in length and often considerably smaller. They may be brightly and strikingly coloured, and males and females usually have a different colour pattern. They are generally ground-dwelling, typically found in leaf litter and under decaying vegetation. They eat small invertebrates, termites and snails being a favourite food. Females lay one egg at a time, which may be very large in relation to their body size, and can be seen through the ventral body wall. They may be present in very high population densities, but are often overlooked because of their small size and secretive habits. They are most active at dusk and dawn, and these are the best times to see them.

The genus *Thecadactylus,* by contrast, are large sized geckos, reaching 120 mm SVL. The Latin name means 'vase-toed' and refers to the shape of the toe pad. They are vocal lizards, calling mainly when they are active at night. There is only one species in the genus, and it is widespread in South and Central America as well as in the

Lesser Antilles. The turnip-tailed gecko, *T. rapicauda,* uses its tail to store fat, hence it has a rather disproportionately swollen shape. It readily sheds its tail to escape predators, and most lizards seen have regenerated tails. It is variable in colour (pale to dark grey, to deep orange) and individuals can change colour from day to night, and possibly also their physiological condition. This may explain why they often seem to match their background. While these lizards are mainly insect feeders, they have been known occasionally to take juvenile *Anolis* and *Sphaerodactylus.* During the day they shelter in deep crevices and rock piles, but may occasionally be seen basking on exposed perches. Their call is a series of chirps, diminishing in loudness. They often display aggression with tail waving, and have a very fragile skin that may be used as an escape strategy.

One endemic species of the genus *Phyllodactylus* (leaf-toed geckos) is recorded but may be extinct.

Family Scincidae

Skinks are usually cylindrical animals with a shiny appearance, and can be arboreal, terrestrial or burrowing. Many have reduced limbs, and some have lost them altogether. Skinks are a large family of lizards (with over 1300 species) which occur all over the warmer regions of the world, but have a mainly eastern hemisphere distribution. Only one genus, *Mabuya,* is present in South America, and in the Lesser Antilles there is only one species, *M. bistriata* (formerly known as *M. mabouya*)[6].

Family Teiidae

Teiids are restricted to the Americas. They are divided into the macroteiids, which may reach very large sizes, and the microteiids (considered by some to consist of a separate family, Gymnophthalmidae). Macroteiids are represented in the Lesser Antilles by the genus *Ameiva* and a single representative each of *Cnemidophorus* (see Conservation) and *Kentropyx.* Most species have large, regular scales on the head and granular body scales, with rectangular ventral scales. Limbs are usually well developed. They are mostly diurnal, ground-dwelling lizards. They feed on birds, small mammals, other lizards, insects and plant material. Eggs are laid in soft soil or termite nests, though some species are parthenogenetic. The microteiids are represented by two species of the genus *Gymnophthalmus,* and a single species of the South American genus *Bachia.* These microteiids are generally small, inconspicuous animals that are often overlooked; they have reduced limbs. Unlike the macroteiids, males are smaller than females.

Family Anguidae

There is a single representative of this family in the Lesser Antilles, *Diploglossus montisserrati*, representing something of a biogeographic enigma. Members of this widely distributed family of lizards have a covering of bony-plated scales that give them a rigid appearance, and the tail is usually long and fragile. Some species are fossorial and have reduced limbs and eyes (although the latter remain fully functional), and others are arboreal and have prehensile tails, often living in epiphytes in rain forest canopies. All species tend to be secretive in their habits. Anguids may lay eggs (some species are known to brood them) and others bear living young.

◆ *Snakes*

Snakes are closely related to lizards, but differ from them in lacking limbs, eyelids and external ears. Most are terrestrial but some are highly specialised for life in trees, soil or water (either fresh water or sea, although there are no sea snakes in the Atlantic or Caribbean). All snakes are predators and feed on relatively large prey, which they swallow whole, being able to dissociate their jawbones. The Lesser Antilles, as is typical of small oceanic islands, has a depauperate snake fauna with only 9 genera and 21 species represented.

Families Typhlopidae and Leptotyphlopidae

Blind snakes (*Typhlops* and *Ramphotyphlops)* and thread snakes (*Leptotyphlops*) are primitive, burrowing (fossorial) snakes with small heads (which are the same diameter as the rest of their body) and reduced eyes. They resemble earthworms more than snakes and are often collectively called worm snakes. The families differ in having teeth only in, respectively, the upper or lower jaws. They have a pan-tropical distribution, but are infrequently seen because of their habit of burrowing and living under rocks, vegetation and logs in generally damp conditions. They are reported to eat predominantly ants and termites and reproduce by laying a few elongated eggs, although some species bear live young. One species, *R. braminus*, recently recorded from Anguilla, is the only confirmed parthenogenetic snake. This species now has a worldwide distribution in the tropics and subtropics, apparently as a result of accidental introductions by man.

Family Boidae

Boas are a group of non-venomous constricting snakes, found in both eastern and western hemispheres, often growing to a large size. They are considered to be relatively primitive snakes, and males still retain vestiges of hindlimbs which are only visible on the exterior as spurs or claws. There are two genera in the Lesser Antilles, *Boa* and *Corallus*, each represented by a single species.

Boa constrictor has two subspecies that are endemic to the Lesser Antilles (from Dominica and St Lucia). A further subspecies is found on a few Caribbean islands and adjacent areas of Central and South America. They are slender snakes when young, but large individuals become increasingly heavy bodied. They eat a wide variety of food including *Ameiva*, rats, bats, agoutis and birds. When mating, boa constrictors form breeding balls or 'cabals' **(3)** where one female attracts several males. They bear live young (as do all boas), 16 young being removed from one specimen in Dominica although up to 80 young are known in captive specimens. Although these slow moving, harmless snakes eat agricultural pests such as rats, they are unfortunately frequently killed, often out of misplaced fear but sometimes for their fat (see Conservation).

The genus *Corallus* is also widespread throughout South and Central America. *C. hortulanus* (formerly known as *C. enydris*)[6] is a

3. Breeding ball of boa constrictors, *Boa constrictor* (St Lucia). The female is larger than the males

largely arboreal, nocturnal snake and although mainland populations prey mainly on endotherms (birds and mammals), the island populations have been found to rely mainly on ectotherms[6] (lizards and frogs).

Family Colubridae

Colubrids are a large group of advanced snakes (containing over 70 per cent of all snake species) with an almost worldwide distribution. Most have a slender, tapering body with a distinct head, usually covered with large, plate-like scutes, the arrangement of which can be an important aid to their identification. Those in the Lesser Antilles (13 species) are medium sized, often terrestrial and partly diurnal. Consequently, they are sensitive to predation by introduced mongoose and some populations are extinct or endangered (see Conservation). Some colubrids, although they lack specialised venom-delivery apparatus (fangs), do produce toxic oral secretions. This secretion is normally delivered to the prey by chewing during an attack. Colubrids do not normally deliver venom during an ordinary defensive bite. Some of the Eastern Caribbean species fall into this category (e.g. *Clelia*, *Liophis*) but none of them are a threat to humans.

Family Viperidae

Only two representatives of this family are present, both belonging to the South and Central American genus of pit vipers, *Bothrops*[7]. No other venomous snakes occur in the Lesser Antilles. Generally heavy bodied with distinctly triangular heads, pit vipers have erectable, large front fangs which fold back against the roof of the mouth, and a pair of heat-sensing pits located between the eyes and nostrils which aid in the detection of warm predators and prey. They are well camouflaged, 'sit-and-wait' predators and found in the Lesser Antilles. Large gravid females may be terrestrial, but they are often arboreal. Their diet is likely to be largely warm-blooded mammals such as mice, rats, and possibly agoutis and opossums. Their natural enemy in St Lucia would have been the large colubrid *Clelia errabunda*, now extinct (ironically this is likely to have occurred as a result of persecution of snakes as a result of fear of being bitten by its main prey, *Bothrops*). *Bothrops* is reportedly preyed on by the introduced mongoose, but is equally likely to return the favour. A large specimen will have few natural enemies other than man, although domestic (or feral) pigs will also eat smaller individuals.

An Example of a Natural Eastern Caribbean Reptile and Amphibian Community: Dominica

The structure of communities on small oceanic islands is often very simple and is known as depauperate. This means that compared to equivalent sized areas of mainland, or a large island, there are comparatively few species present. The Lesser Antillean islands are no exception. All the species have arrived over the sea, although some may have had help, arriving only with the first human colonisers of the islands. Several waves of colonisation occurred by various Indian groups from South America who might have deliberately carried some species for food (e.g. iguanas) or as accidental stowaways (e.g. geckos and frogs).

Dominica belongs to the younger arc, and is one of the largest Eastern Caribbean islands. However, by most standards it is a small island, being only 45 km long and 16 km at its widest point. It is extremely mountainous, with a maximum altitude of 1447 m and several peaks over 1000 m distributed from the extreme northern to the southern tip. It receives a very high rainfall (7000 mm per year on the highest peaks). The spatial and temporal distribution of rainfall determines the distribution of habitats on the island, with rain forest covering much of the centre of the island. This merges into cloud forests at higher elevations and xerophytic vegetation on the leeward (western or Caribbean) coast, which has both the lowest annual rainfall and the most pronounced dry season. While the vegetation of the windward (eastern or Atlantic) coast shares some species with both the xerophytic woodland and rain forest, it is strongly influenced by the salt-laden onshore winds, which give it a characteristic asymmetric (or 'combed') appearance. Reptiles form a significant part of its fauna, and it is one of the few Lesser Antillean islands that appears to have retained its entire original reptile and amphibian fauna.

There are four species of snakes, none of which is venomous, ten species of lizard and three species of frog. However the conditions on the island allow those few species to occur in great numbers, many more than may occur in more complex communities. There are comparatively few insectivorous birds in these islands, and the *Anolis* lizards have evolved to take over this role. These lizards may reach densities of two lizards per square metre of forest floor[8]. Even though each lizard may be small (adult females weigh 5–8 g, depending on where they come from, while males may weigh between 10 and 21 g), these large densities mean that the total weight of living tissue (biomass) reaches very high values. Other reptiles living in these communities may reach a very large size (e.g. boa constrictors and iguanas weighing several kilograms each) although they may not be common. If we add these, it is possible that the reptile fauna in parts of Dominica has one of the highest recorded reptile biomass per unit area in the world.

Another feature of the Eastern Caribbean island communities is the high degree of endemism, i.e. species that are found on only one island in the chain. This is another feature of oceanic islands, which reflects the fact that these islands are difficult to get to for most terrestrial species, since they have to travel over inhospitable sea in order to get there. Unsurprisingly, it is the animals with least ability to disperse over long distances that often show these patterns of endemism. Since only a small number of animals of any species are likely to make up the colonising party, the chances that they are not a random sample of their original species are quite high. As they multiply and spread in their new home, they are likely to face different challenges from those faced in their original home, and, over time, will change in order to meet these challenges, resulting in speciation. However, unlike the mainland or much larger islands, which have many more species present, the species on these islands have not had to avoid competition by specialising in a particular way of life. Some species have spread into a variety of different habitats and have very flexible lifestyles, being equally at home in rain forest or xeric woodland. A particularly striking example is the endemic *Anolis* lizard, *A. oculatus*. This lizard looks so different in the different habitats that it is often mistaken for a different species. In rain forest, it is quite large and is often deep green in colour, scattered with many bluish white spots (4). On the littoral east coast (5), it is intermediate in size and deep orange to chocolate brown in colour, again with many scattered white spots. Here the lizards also have very deep tail crests. On the western,

Caribbean, coast the lizards may be much smaller and paler, being light tan to yellow in ground colour. They also vary in the amount of white markings. Those in the south are rather plain **(6)** while those in the north are extensively stippled and marbled with white patches **(7)**, and often have large black patches on their sides (these descriptions apply to the males; females **(5, 8)** follow the same trends but are less colourful and obvious). They show variation in other aspects of their biology as well, notably in their activity patterns, behaviour and diet. This species has been the subject of intensive study to attempt to understand the cause of this variation[9].

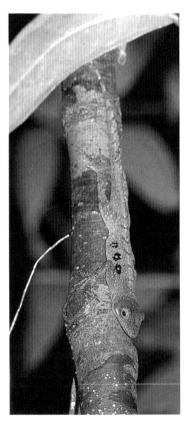 

4. Male Dominican anole, *Anolis oculatus,* from northern rain forest at Syndicate, Dominica

5. Copulating pair of Dominican anoles, *Anolis oculatus,* from Atlantic coast littoral forest, Dominica

6. Male Dominican anole, *Anolis oculatus*, from southern xeric (Caribbean) woodland (Petite Coulibri, Dominica)

7. Male Dominican anole, *Anolis oculatus,* from northern xeric (Caribbean) woodland (Cabrits, Dominica)

8. Female Dominican anole, *Anolis oculatus,* from northern rain forest at Syndicate, Dominica

The reptile and amphibian communities of Dominica will be described from two main sites that are readily accessible. One of these, the Cabrits National Park, is an area of coastal xeric woodland and contains most of the reptile species present on the island. However, there are a few which are only found in moister habitats, and these will be described from the slopes of Morne Diablotin, the highest mountain in Dominica and, at 1447 m, the second highest mountain in the Eastern Caribbean.

THE CABRITS NATIONAL PARK

This National Park is situated on a headland, which was virtually treeless during the eighteenth and nineteenth centuries when the British built and manned Fort Shirley. The trees that now form one of the best examples of xeric woodland **(9)** in the Eastern Caribbean have only grown in the last hundred or so years since the fort was abandoned. The headland takes its name from the feral goats (*cabrit* in French) which were introduced in colonial times to provide food for passing sailors. There is still a small population that

9. Xeric woodland habitat at Cabrits on the northern Caribbean coast of Dominica

evades continuing attempts to exterminate them, but they are at least under control.

This vegetation type occurs in areas of low rainfall (< 2000 mm) with a pronounced dry season. Cabrits consists of two low hills with a maximum elevation of 180 m. It has an average annual temperature of 26 °C and an average annual rainfall of 1870 mm with five months being classified as dry. There is no permanent water on the Cabrits. However, it is far from arid, with a mean relative humidity of around 80 per cent. The vegetation is characterised by deciduous species, which shed their leaves during the dry season. There are few epiphytes except in localised areas where a moister microclimate may occur, such as on the inland slope of east Cabrits where they include orchids such as *Oncidium* sp., eyelash orchid *Epidendrum ciliari*, and bromeliads, e.g. the airplant *Tillandsia* and *Pitcairnia augustifolia*. The trees are generally unbuttressed and may reach a height of 8–12 m. The canopy is fairly complete, and little sunlight reaches the forest floor except during the dry season when most trees will shed their leaves. More than 40 species of tree have been identified, many of which have been traditionally utilised for charcoal, shingles and furniture[10]. Almost all this vegetation throughout the Caribbean has been disturbed at some time, and it is unclear how closely it resembles the original vegetation. There are certainly a large number of introduced species that now flourish. At Cabrits, this includes areas of plantation that were established in the 1950s, with species including blue mahoe (a member of the *Hibiscus* genus) and large-leafed mahogany (of Honduran origin, now apparently invading xeric woodland) and teak.

Significant tree species (with their local names) include *Lonchocarpus latifolius* (savonnet), which forms one of the dominant species at Cabrits, and white cedar *Tabebuia heterophylla* (powye), which often grows right to the edge of the sea but is now relatively uncommon at Cabrits, probably due to past exploitation as it is an excellent timber tree. Others include *Pimenta racemosa* (bwa denn or bay) with its glossy, aromatic leaves and naked Indian, *Bursera simarouba* (gommier wouj), also known as birch gum or turpentine tree for its resinous sap, and as 'tourist tree' for its papery, reddish brown outer bark which naturally peels away to reveal the deep green underbark. Strangling fig *Ficus citrifolia* (figuier) is mainly restricted to the ruins at Cabrits. Shrubby species include *Croton*, lepiné (*Zanthoxylum spinosum* or *caribaeum*), *Leucida leucocephala* (a legume) and *Morinda citrifolia* (a large leafed plant with knobbly, fleshy fruit). Another characteristic feature of xeric woodland is the presence of thorny species, e.g. the sand box tree *Hura crepitans* (sabliye), silk cotton tree *Ceiba pentandra* (fomaje) and logwood *Haematoxylon campechianum* (kampech). Thorny shrubs include *Acacia* and *Lantana* species. Succulent plants include 'leaf-of-life' (*Bryophyllum* sp.). On the outer slopes near the sea, the effects of wind and sea spray, especially on the northern side, modify the vegetation. Species here include white cedar, Indian almond (*Terminalia capitata*), sea grape (*Cocoloba uvifera*), the poisonous manchineel (*Hippomane mancinella*) and seaside mahoe (*Thespesia populanaea*)[11].

Land crabs are also common here. The hermit or soldier crab (*Coenobita cylpeatus*) is most easily seen, and burrows of the larger crabs (the black crab *Gegarcinus ruricola* and the touloulou *G. lateralis*) may be seen during the day. The crabs themselves are only easily seen at night when they are out foraging. This is also when they fall prey to the yellow-crowned night heron, whose handiwork can be seen in the form of the many empty crab shells, with a hole in the carapace where the beak was driven through, which litter the paths. The remnants of their meals may in turn be food for the scavenging ground lizards (*Ameiva fuscata*). Termites and ants are abundant and are very important in the rapid recycling of nutrients in dry habitats where decomposition of plant material is slow. Insectivorous lizards **(10)** play an important role in passing on this resource to higher levels of the food chain. This is especially true of the anole *Anolis oculatus*, which in spite of being well adapted for an arboreal lifestyle, forage mainly on the ground. In spite of their relatively large size, the bulk of their diet in xeric woodland consists of tiny ants and termites. Termites are also a staple item of the diet of the extremely small, terrestrial, dwarf gecko, *Sphaerodactylus fantasticus,* which, although not particularly abundant at this site, may reach very high population densities in xeric woodland. These lizards then fall prey to other reptiles such as the racer *Alsophis antillensis* **(11)** and are also preyed upon by birds **(12)** such as the mangrove cuckoo, kingbird and pearly-eyed thrasher, whose characteristic calls can commonly be heard at the Cabrits. The most striking thing about the reptile community at Cabrits, however, is its sheer abundance (frogs, *Eleutherodactylus martinicensis* **(13, 14)**, are only present in relatively low densities in this dry area).

Some of the most obvious inhabitants are the tree lizards (*Anolis oculatus*) **(6, 11)**. Almost every tree and sapling will have its tree lizard perched head down, scanning the ground for food or for other lizards. They are comparatively tame at this site and will

10. Male Dominican anole, *Anolis oculatus,* feeding on a cockroach

11. A racer, *Alsophis antillensis,* devouring a female Dominican anole at Cabrits, Dominica

12. Male Dominican anole, *Anolis oculatus* (Petite Coulibri, Dominica), showing a peck mark on the trunk from an attack by an avian predator (probably a king bird)

13. Whistling frog, *Eleutherodactylus martinicensis* (Pointe Baptiste, Dominica)

14. Whistling frog, *Eleutherodactylus martinicensis* (Trois Rivières, Guadeloupe)

allow a close approach before disappearing up the tree. Anoles are active throughout the day, at a wide range of temperatures, but activity (especially feeding) is greatest during the cooler parts of the day, at dawn and dusk. At night, they retreat to the tips of branches and sleep while clinging to leaves **(15)** where they are safe

15. A sleeping female Dominican anole, *Anolis oculatus* (Picard, Dominica)

from heavier nocturnal predators. Males guard their territories throughout the day, perching in an obvious position, which makes them very vulnerable to predation, and displaying at potential rivals (or mates) by raising and lowering their dewlaps. They may also use a 'push-up' display, and if the intruder persists and a confrontation takes place at close quarters, the lizards inflate themselves to look larger and gape menacingly. On a few occasions, physical contact may be made, but this rarely lasts long or results in serious injury. Research has shown that in such confrontations, the resident male usually wins, even if it is smaller than the intruding male. Females also have territories, which they defend, but these are smaller than the territories of males. This means that a male's territory will overlap with that of more than one female, and these females will usually mate with him. Females are oviparous, only carrying a single egg at a time. When the egg is almost ready to be laid, it can be clearly seen through the ventral body wall. Eggs are laid under rocks, leaves, bark, etc. In captivity, females have produced eggs every 14 days. Although they breed throughout the year, there is a peak towards the end of the dry season, especially in the more seasonal areas such as Cabrits.

16. Adult male Dominican ground lizard, *Ameiva fuscata* (Cabrits, Dominica)

Ground lizards (*Ameiva fuscata*) are also abundant and easily seen because of their size. This species is endemic to Dominica and although many of its relatives have been driven extinct on neighbouring islands, it continues to flourish in Dominica (see Conservation). They are often heard rustling through the undergrowth just off the paths as they move jerkily though the litter foraging for fallen fruit, carrion and invertebrates. They are heliothermic and are usually only observed during the hottest part of the day, and may not be active at all in bad weather. Males grow to larger sizes than females, reaching 200 mm SVL. There is little sexual dimorphism in colour and so the sexes can only be told apart with difficulty. Adult males **(16)** have broader heads (especially the jowls) than females, and tend to be more uniformly bluish grey in colour. However, juveniles **(17)** of both sexes look very different from adults, and are impossible to sex from their external appearance. They are an attractive coppery-brown colour, though not as shiny as skinks or microteiids **(18a, 18b, 18c)**. There is a dark-brown lateral stripe on each side, the borders of which are marked by yellow lines, which fade towards the rear. There are also yellow lateral spots and flecks on the lateral stripes, which turn blue as the

17. Juvenile Dominican ground lizard, *Ameiva fuscata* (Cabrits, Dominica)

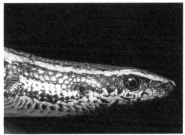

a

b

18. A comparison of the heads of three lizard species which could possibly be confused with each other: (a) juvenile *Ameiva fuscata*; (b) *Gymnophthalmus pleei*; (c) *Mabuya bistriata* (all from xeric woodland in north Dominica)

c

animal matures, as does the rest of the body. However, the dorsal surface is heavily flecked with black, giving it an overall greyish blue appearance. The ventral surface, pinkish in the juveniles, becomes pale blue, washed on the throat and chest with dark blue-grey. The inner thighs are vividly spotted with bright blue spots. Some smaller individuals have reddish brown dorsal surfaces[12]. It is found throughout the island in cultivated areas and xeric woodland. It can also live at quite high altitudes in open cultivated areas, as it requires patches of direct sunlight in which to bask in order to reach the high body temperatures at which it operates (it is often observed basking on the edge of the road). It reproduces throughout the year, laying three to seven eggs, the clutch size being correlated with the size of the female. These lizards are relatively wary, and will make off at speed, sometimes raising the front part of their body slightly off the ground and running bipedally.

Ameiva fuscata is a macroteiid, but its smaller microteiid relatives are also present here. Microteiids are extremely elongated animals (most of which is tail) with relatively short limbs, reaching only around 50 mm SVL. They resemble the skink *Mabuya bistriata* (see below) much more than their larger relatives; however, they have relatively larger heads **(18)** and only four toes on the front legs. They are metallic brown dorsally, with a golden yellow stripe starting at the snout and passing over each eye on to the body, and fading shortly after the level of the forelimb. The sides are dark grey-brown or reddish brown, and the ventral surface may be dark or pale with grey-black markings. Only one species, *Gymnophthalmus pleei* **(18b, 19)**, has been officially recorded, but there is considerable variability in the scale counts of individuals caught in the south and north of the island, and it is very likely that another species, *G. underwoodi*, is also present. These species look very similar, and are separated by characters such as the degree of keeling of body scales (*G. underwoodi* having unkeeled body scales, while those of G. *pleei* are keeled towards the posterior) and number of dorsal scale rows at mid-body (the former having 13 and the latter usually 17–19). G. *underwoodi* is unisexual and reproduces parthenogenetically, and captive specimens have been recorded laying up to 11 eggs in a four-month period, each clutch being one to four eggs. Juveniles are only 16–19 mm long when newly hatched. Like their larger relatives, they are also diurnal heliotherms, and hence are restricted to relatively open, sunlit areas, mostly coastal. One (unidentified species) was recently sighted at relatively high altitude (300 m) on the slopes of Morne Diablotin, in a banana plantation. However, at this altitude they are likely to be active during a very restricted number of days in the year.

The skink, *Mabuya bistriata* **(18c, 20)**, is bronze or copper-coloured with a darker brown stripe on its sides, which may be bordered by cream lines. Sexes are difficult to tell apart although females reach a larger size (to 93 mm SVL) and adult males in

19. *Gymnophthalmus pleei* (xeric woodland, north Dominica), a microteiid

20. *Mabuya bistriata* (Dominica) is the only skink species found in these islands

breeding condition develop a rose-pink flush on their throats. Although basically terrrestrial, they are good climbers and may be seen in trees and in the roofs of buildings as well as on the ground. They are diurnal and heliothermic, depending on frequent basking to maintain the high body temperature required for activity. They therefore tend to be seen during the middle of the day only, and may not be active at all on overcast and wet days. They are active foragers, hunting for arthropods (mainly insects and woodlice). Their movement is sinuous and smooth, unlike that of *Gymnophthalmus*, which is more skittery. It can also be distinguished from the latter by having overlapping head scales **(18)**. *M. bistriata* is ovoviviparous, giving birth to three to five young which are born 36–48 hours apart. On many islands, its numbers have been reduced by mongoose predation (see Conservation).

The gecko family is represented at Cabrits by the large and abundant turnip-tailed gecko *Thecadactylus rapicauda* **(21, 22)**. However, being nocturnal, they often escape notice as they shelter in crevices of trees and houses. Its much smaller relative *Sphaerodactylus fantasticus* **(23)**, which is also found on the neighbouring islands of Guadeloupe, Îles des Saintes, Marie Galante and Montserrat, is actually respectably sized for a dwarf gecko, reaching 29 mm SVL. It is found along the length of the dry western coast of the island but does not appear to be present on the east coast. While this may be simply because it has not been found there, surveys have been undertaken of suitable habitat without

21. Adult turnip-tailed gecko, *Thecadactylus rapicauda* (Dominica)

22. Juvenile turnip-tailed gecko, *Thecadactylus rapicauda* (Dominica)

23. Adult male dwarf gecko, *Sphaerodactylus fantasticus* (xeric woodland, Dominica)

locating it. Even on the west coast, only a few localities are known which support large populations of these lizards. Males are striking animals, having sharply demarcated deep blue heads with scattered light blue spots. Females are duller, usually with two stripes forming an upside-down V on the back of the head, and continuing as stripes down the body. They appear very similar morphologically to the populations from the vicinity of the capital Basse Terre in Guadeloupe, and recent molecular studies have shown that they are genetically identical, thus suggesting that they are very recent colonists of Dominica, almost certainly having been brought there through the agency of man.

The Lesser Antillean iguana *I. delicatissima* **(24, 25)** may occasionally be seen, although it is not the best place to expect to see them on the island. They are primarily found on the coast but have occasionally been seen at rain forest sites. They frequent cliff faces as well as trees, and their diet includes prickly pear fruit, birds' eggs and carrion as well as the leaves, flowers and fruit of more than fifty species of trees and bushes from the xeric coastal woodland. They may be important seed-dispersal agents in this ecosystem.

24. Female Lesser Antillean iguana, *Iguana delicatissima* (La Désirade)

25. Male Lesser Antillean iguana, *Iguana delicatissima* (St Barts)

They spend a great deal of their time thermoregulating by moving between perches in the sun and shade, and even sleep in the crowns of trees. When necessary, they move between trees by leaping between them, and are therefore rarely seen on the ground. However, female iguanas lay their eggs in burrows dug in soft, sandy ground **(26)**, and are often killed by cars as they cross the coast road towards the beaches. As many as 18 eggs are laid in August to October, and the young hatch three months later. If they survive natural hazards, they may live up to 20 years.

All the snake species present in Dominica can be found at the Cabrits. The snake *Alsophis antillensis* **(11, 27)** is common and may frequently be seen foraging, especially in the mornings and late

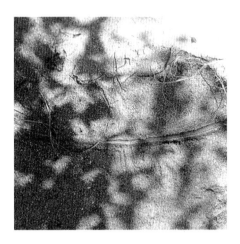

26. The tail of a female Lesser Antillean iguana protruding from her nesting burrow (La Désirade)

27. Male racer, *Alsophis antillensis* (Dominica)

afternoons. Lizards (especially *Anolis*) are likely to form a large part of its diet at this site, and it also eats small rodents. It reaches almost a metre in length, with large white to light brown blotches on a chocolate to dark brown background often alternating to form a zigzag which grades into a more dark uniform dorsum posteriorly. Females are usually lighter brown than males. The Dominican subspecies is endemic, although other subspecies are found on the nearby islands of Montserrat and the Guadeloupean Archipelago. It is widespread in Dominica but is most common in xeric woodland. It lays several eggs (five are reported). It rarely bites, but may release a foul-smelling cloacal secretion. It is frequently killed on sight, although it is completely harmless.

Another colubrid, the grove snake *Liophis juliae* **(28)**, is also present, though less often observed. It is an attractive snake, up to half

28. Grove snake,
Liophis juliae
(Syndicate, Dominica)

a metre long, often with white to yellowish flecks or spots on a glossy dark background (sometimes described as a 'salt-and-pepper' pattern). However, some specimens (especially in montane areas) may be uniformly dark. The Dominican subspecies is endemic, although other subspecies are found on the nearby islands of Guadeloupe and Marie Galante. This species is widespread across Dominica. It is diurnal and an active forager, eating lizards, frogs and insects. It may lay from two to four eggs. Birds such as the broad-winged hawk are its main predators. Like *Alsophis* it will release a foul-smelling cloacal secretion, but otherwise is a gentle and inoffensive snake.

Boa constrictors *Boa constrictor* **(3, 29)** may grow up to 3 m (males are smaller) but are more frequently seen at less than half this length. They have 23–35 rectangular or irregular transverse markings on their dorsal trunk against a grey-brown to dark brown

29. Boa constrictor,
Boa constrictor
(Hampstead,
Dominica)

30. Dominican blind snake, *Typhlops dominicana* (Dominica)

background. Dominican boas differ from others in lacking a red tail. They are widespread across the island, being found in most habitats from coastal xeric and littoral woodland as well as in montane rain forest. They are more active by night than day and are often seen dead on the road in the morning, particularly on some northern Caribbean coastal roads.

The Dominican blind snake *Typhlops dominicana* **(30)** reaches 385 mm in total length, with only a very small part of this being tail. It has a small rounded head and is mid- to dark-brown on its dorsal surface, generally having a lighter ventral surface, particularly around the head and tail. This subspecies is endemic to Dominica, but another subspecies is found on the adjacent island of Guadeloupe. It is widespread in Dominica but not often seen because of its secretive habits. It is more likely to be seen in the open in the early morning, especially after heavy rain at night. Otherwise, it can sometimes be found by turning over rotting logs (these should always be replaced in their original position afterwards).

MORNE DIABLOTIN AND THE SYNDICATE NATURE TRAIL

The nature trail at Syndicate Estate is situated on the slopes of Morne Diablotin at an altitude of *c*. 640 m. It receives an average annual rainfall of 5620 mm, and has an average annual temperature of only 22 °C. The average humidity is over 85 per cent, and there are no dry months. The vegetation here is lower montane rain forest **(31)**. Over 60 species with girth at breast height (gbh) more than 10 cm have been recorded per 1000 m². *Dacryodes excelsea* (locally called gommier) is the dominant tree species, along with three species of *Sloanea* (chatagnier). A signpost along the nature trail indicates one fine example of the latter (small-leafed chatagnier). The shrub *Cephaelis schwartzii,* with waxy blue bracts surrounding small white flowers, is the most common ground-layer shrub. Filmy ferns are abundant and tree ferns are also present. Terrestrial orchids with purple flowers may also be found, but the arboreal orchids are on the branches of the trees so far above the ground that they are seldom seen unless a tree has fallen. There is an abundance of lianas, climbers (chiefly aroids) and epiphytes, e.g. large-leafed anthuriums, are present. Many

31. Rain forest habitat at Syndicate, north Dominica

epiphytes, e.g. bromeliads, are up in the sunlit canopy, where in spite of the abundant rainfall they display xerophytic adaptation because of their exposed positions. Epiphytic shrubs, especially species of *Clusia*, occur in various stages towards eventual strangulation of their host.

Most people visit Syndicate hoping to catch a glimpse of the two species of endemic parrots (red-necked and imperial)[13]. However, this is also a good place to see montane reptiles and amphibians. *Anolis oculatus* **(4, 8)** are relatively abundant but hard to see, being very cryptically coloured to resemble the mossy tree trunks on which they are mostly to be found. The best time to see them is in the early morning and late afternoon, when they descend from high perches to feed on the ground and display to each other, often continuing until it is too dark to see them without a torch. At midday they are inactive, although males may still be visible on the trunks of trees as they stake out their territories. At these rain forest sites, the lizards have very different diets from those of their relatives in xeric woodlands such as Cabrits[14], eating much larger and more soft-bodied food items. *Eleutherodactylus* frogs are also abundant and may be heard (and sometimes seen) after rain during the day, and at night. Dominica has two species of whistling frogs (*Eleutherodactylus*) which are not very readily distinguished as they are both relatively small and have rather similar, variable, colour patterns. *Eleutherodactylus martinicensis* **(13, 14)** is quite large for a whistling frog, the females having a SVL of 47 mm. The dorsal background colour varies considerably, ranging from reddish brown, yellow-brown, dark brown and grey with red on the hindlimbs and groin. The dorsal pattern is also variable and often includes a dark interocular bar and one or two dark chevrons. There may be a wide vertebral stripe, pale dorsolateral stripes and a single wide crural crossbar. The ventral surface is pale, often with numerous dark stippling while the throat is pale with distinct dark spots[15]. In Dominica the glandular vocal sac is bronze to gold. This species is distributed in the Central Lesser Antilles from Antigua to Martinique and in Dominica it is found from sea level to 800 m elevation. Gelatinous eggs (*c*. 30–40) are laid in, or under, vegetation. At this site, it is likely to be the common species *E. martinicensis* that is heard, but the endemic *E. amplinympha* (which was only described in 1994)[16] is present at higher altitudes, and over an elevational range of 50–100 m the two species may exist side by side. Although at other sites on the island *E. amplinympha* **(32)** has been found at elevations of *c*. 400 m, on the slopes of Morne Diablotin it

32. The endemic whistling frog, *Eleutherodactylus amplinympha*, from Fresh Water Lake, Dominica

has only been found much higher than Syndicate, on the trail to the top of the mountain[17], where the vegetation changes to true montane or cloud forest. In montane forest, the canopy becomes lower and the forest less stratified. The air is extremely humid, with moisture often condensing directly out of the air on to the vegetation. There is usually an abundant layer of vegetation on the ground, and mosses and filmy ferns adorn every available surface. There are many bromeliads growing on (or close to) the ground, and these form excellent breeding sites for *E. amplinympha* **(33)**.

However, the two species are not easy to identify, as both are very variable in colour pattern. The inner two toes on the front feet of *amplinympha* are equal in size, but are different in size in *martinicensis* and *johnstonei*. Exceptionally large individuals (over 50 mm SVL) are likely to be female *E. amplinympha,* which is the largest species of this genus in the Lesser Antilles. Auditory identification may also be possible. *E. martinicensis* has a two-part call, with a short level note followed by a longer rising note. This may alternate with a series of rapid clicks. The latter are more frequently given at the beginning and end of the calling periods and may serve as a location signal to other males, while the two-part whistle is

a

b

33. (a) Bromeliads in montane rain forest collect water in the central tank and are used as nesting sites by *Eleutherodactylus amplinympha*
(b) A clutch of eggs laid *by E. amplinympha* in the above bromeliad, Fresh Water Lake, Dominica

mainly an advertisement call to attract females. *E. amplinympha* also uses a series of clicks in a similar way, but its advertisement call has an extra note at the end of the rising whistle, making it a three-part call. The only sure way to tell them apart is to look at their biochemistry.

Many endemic species of *Eleutherodactylus*, all over the Lesser Antilles, are restricted to montane forests, and appear to be unable to coexist with the more widespread *E. martinicensis* and *E. johnstonei* (see below). It has been noted that the distribution of these latter two species almost perfectly matches the boundaries of the former colonial trading routes[18], and it is possible that these are 'weed' species, that are better than the endemic species at occupying disturbed agricultural areas.

The snakes *Boa constrictor* and *Liophis juliae* are infrequently encountered at Syndicate, although they may be very common in localised areas. The latter often lack bold white markings at these high elevations and are plain black or dark brown. Agoutis (rodents) are sometimes seen in late afternoon, and these may form part of the diet of boas, as might the many rats that inhabit the cultivated edges of the forest. The gecko *Thecadactylus rapicauda* **(21, 22)** is also found (although at lower densities than in xeric woodland) at quite high altitudes on the edges of the forest, in banana or cattle sheds, and even hiding in the hollow metal tubes used to construct interpretative signs at Syndicate. There is a different species of dwarf gecko, *S. vincenti* **(34)**, at Syndicate. Although on the other islands on which it is also found (including Martinique, St Lucia and St Vincent) it occupies a range of habitats including xeric scrub, in Dominica it is confined to the wet mountains. It has been found at a variety of locations including Syndicate, ranging from 400 to 900 m in altitude. It is usually seen

34. Male dwarf gecko, *Sphaerodactylus vincenti* (Syndicate, Dominica)

35. Mountain chicken, *Leptodactylus fallax* (Springfield, Dominica)

on the ground but has also been recorded from the leaves of high bromeliads[19]. In Dominica, males have a dark-bordered eyespot (ocellus) on each shoulder and it is larger than *S. fantasticus* **(23)**, with both sexes reaching 40 mm. Not much is known about its habits but they are likely to be similar to other dwarf geckos.

Although not present as high as Syndicate, the mountain chicken *Leptodactylus fallax* **(35)** may be heard on descending the mountain at dusk. Despite its common name, it is a large frog (females reach 17 cm SVL). This species is frequently used for food, and its name derives from the fact that it tastes rather like chicken. More recently it is becoming widely used as a novelty food for tourism, with an unknown impact upon the population (see Conservation). This frog has marked dorsolateral folds from the eye to the groin and a reddish orange background colour. The male has a thumb spine, which is used to grip the female during mating. It is more frequently heard than seen, and has a very loud, whooping call given at intervals of roughly 1 second[20]. It calls primarily from April to September, particularly along watercourses and the call is probably used to 'mark' territory. It is also found on Montserrat. On Dominica it is found from sea level to *c.* 300 m altitude only on the western side of the island, in natural forest and agricultural areas. This species is a nocturnal 'sit-and-wait' predator which is reported to prey primarily on crickets, beetles, slugs, snails, millipedes and decapod crustaceans, while it occasionally eats vertebrates such as *Eleutherodactylus, Anolis,* boas and even bats[21]. Twenty or so eggs are laid in a foam nest in a burrow half a metre long, which is guarded by the female[22].

OTHER SPECIES

Hemidactylus mabouia **(36, 37)** is largely found around human habitation, being a true 'house gecko', and is not very abundant in Dominica. It and its relatives are now found across the tropical regions of the world, having been dispersed by either (or both) natural and human-aided processes. They are pale and inconspicuous

36. House gecko, *Hemidactylus mabouia*. This heavily marked specimen was found under bark in xeric woodland (Antigua)

37. House gecko, *Hemidactylus mabouia*. This lightly marked specimen was found in a house (Dominica)

38. A captive specimen of the tortoise *Geochelone carbonaria* (Dominica)

lizards, reaching 68 mm SVL and lacking a loud voice. The ground colour is greyish white to light brown, often with light- to dark-brown V-shaped bands (especially in juveniles) pointing backwards towards the tail, which may also be banded. It has some ability to change colour. Unlike parts of Asia, where there may be several house geckos in each room, it does not seem to be very abundant on Eastern Caribbean islands. While usually found near houses, they can also be seen in rock piles and under bark. They lay their eggs in crevices and the young hatch at only 21 mm SVL. They may be diurnal as well as nocturnal.

The tortoise *Geochelone carbonaria* **(38)** has been recorded from Dominica, although it was probably a recent introduction. Although the occasional specimen may be encountered, these are possibly escaped pets and it is extremely unlikely that a viable natural population exists. It is quite large, with a rather flat-topped oval carapace up to half a metre long. The carapace is black with yellow markings on each shield (although all-yellow individuals have also been recorded). It is oval in shape in younger animals, becoming elongated in older ones. The plastron is dull yellow with black markings. The head may have bright yellow postorbital streaks and areas of the tail and feet are red (or may be orange or yellow).

The seas around Dominica are also home to an ancient group of marine reptiles – sea turtles. Green, hawksbill, loggerhead and leatherback turtles may all be seen although the commonest and most likely to be encountered are the hawksbills **(2)**. Turtles are occasionally taken for food by local spear-fishermen, but nests are not usually raided. Nesting on Dominica is likely to be an occasional event, as there are few suitable sandy beaches (some of these include Picard, Douglas Bay, Toucari and Hampstead) which may vary in size or presence depending on hurricanes.

Several checklists of the reptiles of Dominica include two species whose presence on Dominica is unlikely or erroneous. One of these, usually referred to as *Clelia clelia* (but now shown to be a different species, *C. errabunda*; see St Lucia) is a colubrid that reaches extremely large size (*c.* 2 m) and is a specialist reptile feeder. It was originally found on one other Lesser Antillean island, St Lucia, where it is now extinct. However, recently it was conclusively shown[23] that the record from Dominica was due to a cataloguing error. Occasional reports by foresters of large 'black' snakes are likely to be melanic boas **(39)**, and even so, juveniles of most *Clelia* species are not black but reddish with a conspicuous yellow collar. As juveniles will be far more abundant than adults, the total lack of sightings of anything corresponding to this should be a clear indication that this snake is not present on Dominica.

The other species whose presence on Dominica is in doubt is *Sphaerodactylus microlepis*. The main range of this species is in St Lucia, and the record for Dominica rests on a single specimen with no precise locality. However, it was catalogued together with some specimens that are clearly from Dominica[24] so it cannot be clearly attributed to an error. Its presence in Dominica, however, remains to be verified.

39. An example of a melanic boa, *Boa constrictor*, from Dominica (captive specimen)

40. Whistling frog, *Eleutherodactylus johnstonei* (Saba)

The presence of a third species of whistling frog, on the other hand, has recently been confirmed[25]. *E. johnstonei* **(40)** is widespread throughout the Lesser Antilles and is a recent introduction on Dominica. It is easy to confuse this species with its close relative *E martinicensis* **(13, 14)**, but *E. johnstonei* is slightly smaller, the females having a maximum SVL of 35 mm. The dorsal colour is grey-brown to brown with usually one or two scapular chevrons often with distinct dorsolateral stripes, no red on the hindlimbs or groin (unlike *E. martinicensis*) and a pale ventral surface with a stippled throat. It gives a long series of weak, whispery two-note whistles[26], which can be given at a rate of 60 per minute. On many islands, *E. martinicensis* appears to be becoming displaced by introduced *E. johnstonei*. However, in Dominica, *E. johnstonei* is restricted to the narrow strip on the sea side of the coast road from Fond Colet to Mahaut, and along the edge of the Imperial Road up the Antrim Valley as far as Springfield[25]. It appears that it can only successfully invade disturbed habitats.

Finally, there is at present the possibility that the reptile list of Dominica may soon have another species added to it. While it has been known for some years that a microteid *Gymnophthalmus* was present (see the Cabrits section above), the original specimens are very variable[27] and it is clear that more than one species is present. However, the taxonomy of *Gymnophthalmus* species is itself a matter that requires resolving[6], so the identities of the species present on Dominica may not be definitively known for some time.

Island Profiles

SOMBRERO

This small, uninhabited and isolated island lies 32 miles north-west of the Anguilla Bank. It is the northernmost island in the Lesser Antilles and is politically part of Anguilla. Between 1860 and 1880, intensive mining for phosphate reduced the island to a low flat rock pockmarked with quarry holes. Further damage to the island's habitat resulted from a severe hurricane in 1898, which was stated by contemporary reports to have swamped the island with seawater. These combined effects may have had substantial impact upon the reptile populations[28]. At present, the island is treeless, supporting cactus and other arid-zone ground flora.

41. Male anole, *Anolis gingivinus* (St Martin)

42. Dwarf gecko, *Sphaerodactylus sputator* (St Martin)

No snakes, amphibians, chelonids (other than marine turtles) or crocodilians have been reported from Sombrero, but there are four lizards present, including an endemic species of *Ameiva, A. corvina*. This species grows to 133 mm SVL (females being considerably smaller than males), and is patternless, being rather plain brown to slaty black in colour. Males have brown flecks on the dorsal surface and distinctly browner heads. The tail is sometimes speckled with green, and the ventral surface is dark green to black, mottled with light blue. Their diet includes the eggs of ground-nesting birds, and it is possible that their melanistic colour pattern is a result of natural selection from the high rate of predation by seabirds upon the relatively exposed lizards[28]. The other species of lizards present are *Anolis gingivinus* **(41)**, *Sphaerodactylus sputator* **(42)** (see the Anguilla section below for a full description of these species) and the turnip-tailed gecko *Thecadactylus rapicauda* **(21, 22)** (described in the Dominica chapter).

ANGUILLA

Anguilla is predominantly limestone and low-lying, and hence is rather arid. Its natural vegetation has been degraded and much of the island is now covered with scrub. There are also a few mangrove swamps, freshwater swamps and saltwater ponds. The Fountain cave area, near Shoal Bay East, retains some natural vegetation. Another good, relatively undisturbed area which has a variety of reptiles is Katouche Bay (between Sandy Ground and the Valley). The island is surrounded by a number of smaller satellites, including Dog Island, Lower and Upper Prickly Pear Cays and Scrub Island.

The presence of the whistling frog *Eleutherodactylus johnstonei* **(40)** (see Dominica) has recently been confirmed[29] at the Agriculture Station (The Valley), and seems to be the result of a recent introduction as previous extensive collecting efforts had failed to find it. The presence of the tortoise *Geochelone carbonaria* **(38)** was suspected but not confirmed until recently[30].

A smaller islet off the satellite Scrub Island, Little Scrub, despite its small size, has recently been found to harbour an endemic species of *Ameiva, A. corax*[28]. This is another melanistic species, and thus superficially resembles *A. corvina* of Sombrero as well as having some similarities in scalation characteristics. This is likely to be a result of independent adaptation to the similar habitats present on both islands. The main island of Anguilla, and its other satellites (except Lower Prickly Pear Cay), is occupied by another species of ground lizard, *A. plei* **(43)**. It is a large species with males reaching 181 mm SVL and females reaching 139 mm, although there is inter-island variation in the maximum size. Adults are grey-brown with a greenish blue tinge, and have white spots along the flanks, which may coalesce into white bars posteriorly. The ventral surface is bluish white to white and is patternless. Juveniles are brown with seven light (sometimes broken) stripes. However, there

43. Ground lizard, *Ameiva plei* (St Martin)

is considerable variation in colour pattern. For example, larger adults tend to lack stripes and only have white to greenish white spots along the flanks and posteriorly on the back. There may also be between-island variation (for example, striped specimens from Scrub Island have more distinct stripes than those from Anguilla itself).

The anole *Anolis gingivinus* **(41)** is widespread and common on the island and its satellites, occurring on almost every scrap of emergent land with more than herb-stage vegetation. In the absence of competition from another species of anole, it occupies a wide range of perch heights on the trunk of trees, and on Lower Prickly Pear Cay where ground lizards are absent, it may also frequently be found on the ground. Another species of anole, *A. pogus* **(44)** (see St Martin), has been introduced on to the small islet of Anguillita as part of an experiment exploring the way similar species share resources[31]. *Anolis gingivinus* is a moderate sized anole, reaching 72 mm SVL (males), with an olive to light green dorsal background colour and a cream to bright yellow belly. There is a broad mid-dorsal stripe and a light stripe on the flank extending from the shoulder to the groin. Males may also be heavily spotted or marbled with grey-brown. It is heavily preyed upon by American kestrels in Anguilla, forming a significant part of their diet[32].

There are two species of *Sphaerodactylus* dwarf geckos on Anguilla, *S. macrolepis* and *S. sputator* **(42)**. The former species is apparently more closely related to Greater Antillean species than to other Lesser Antillean ones, and has its main distribution in Puerto Rico and the US and British Virgin Islands. It is a moderately sized species, reaching *c*. 35 mm (both sexes) with very large and strongly keeled dorsal scales. The dorsum may be patternless tan to brown in males, or have a 'salt-and-pepper' pattern of scattered darker scales. There is usually a scapular dark patch containing a pair of pale white to buff ocelli (which may be reduced or absent). The head is uniformly yellow or yellow-orange. The ventral surface is pale, and there may be markings on the throat. *S. sputator,* which has a widespread distribution throughout the Anguilla and St Kitts Banks, is a similar size, although females have been recorded as reaching the slightly larger size of 39 mm SVL. There is no sexual dichromatism, and in Anguilla the dorsal ground colour is pale pink with a series of five to eight brown-edged pale crossbands on the back, continuing but becoming less defined on the tail. The throat is pale yellow and the ventral colour is creamy white. The iris is golden, and there is a yellow canthal line. The very distinct difference in the colour pattern of the two species will prevent any confusion between them.

The widespread geckos *Hemidactylus mabouia* (**36, 37**) and *T. rapicauda* (**21, 22**) and the skink *M. bistriata* (**18c, 20**) (described in the Dominica chapter) are also present. The endangered *Iguana delicatissima* (**24, 25**) (see Dominica) is still found on Anguilla but seems to be restricted to the Little Bay area. *Iguana iguana* (**45**) (the common iguana, see Saba for a full description) arrived on the island after Hurricane Luis in 1995, and may pose a threat to the continued existence of *I. delicatissima* on this island, the most northerly in its range (see Conservation).

The colubrid *Alsophis rijersmai* is somewhat smaller (*c*. 800 mm SVL) than the Dominican *Alsophis* (see Dominica chapter), with a greenish brown background with a dark lateral headstripe that extends on to the body and then breaks up into a series of small square markings. On the neck there are a pair of dark spots and a band with irregular to diamond markings down the dorsum. This species is found on Anguilla and Scrub Island as well as on the other islands of the Anguilla bank (St Martin and St Barthélemy). It is an active diurnal forager and its main prey is anoles. Another snake species has recently been discovered on the island, the worm snake *Ramphotyphlops braminus*, which was previously unrecorded from the West Indies although widely distributed throughout the tropics.

ST MARTIN

St Martin is split between two countries, the northern part being French and the southern part Dutch (Sint Maarten). The island has mountains reaching 420 m in altitude with moist forest and lower lying areas, which have many salt ponds. It has been heavily developed for tourism and there is little evidence of natural vegetation at lower altitudes. For this reason, reptiles are not particularly abundant all over the island, although they may reach high densities in particularly suitable locations (e.g. in the vegetation behind Mullet Bay beach, and along the trail to Pic du Paradis, the highest point of the island). There is one large satellite island, Tintamarre.

The whistling frog, *Eleutherodactylus johnstonei* (**40**) (see Dominica), is found on St Martin together with *Scinax rubra*. The

44. Male anole, *Anolis pogus* (St Martin)

latter frog is possibly a recent introduction, and can be distinguished from the former by its larger size (up to 44 mm SVL in females) and a long rounded snout which extends beyond the lower jaw, with a flattened body and moderately webbed toes. The dorsal surface is pale grey to brown with light longitudinal markings. Thighs have yellow spots in dark reticulations, the vocal sac is yellow and the iris is bronze with dark reticulations[33]. Calling males are reported to turn very yellow[6], and the call is a mechanical-sounding continuous squeaking (up to 10 notes given in series). It is widespread in the lower elevations of tropical South America and Trinidad, but is only found on one other Lesser Antillean Island (St Lucia). It is a human commensal and prefers open country. Eggs are deposited in shallow pools in the wet season. The terrestrial chelonid, *Geochelone carbonaria* **(38)** (see Dominica) may, questionably, occur.

There are a variety of lizards, including the geckos *H. mabouia* **(36, 37)** and *T. rapicauda* **(21, 22)**, *S. macrolepis* and *S. sputator* **(42)** (see Dominica and Anguilla accounts for descriptions of these species). *S. sputator* in St Martin and its satellites is slightly different in appearance to the Anguilla population. Although the basic pattern is the same, in St Martin it has a sandy to pale tan dorsal background colour with a pearly underside. The tail is pale yellow to orange and the iris is bronze. The ground lizard is *A. plei* **(43)**, and the population from the main island (not including Tintamarre) has recently been described as a new subspecies[28]. It differs most obviously by having faded stripes even in small specimens (to the extent that they may appear plain), and in having three to five vertical black bars or bands across the shoulder region in large specimens.

There are two species of anole on St Martin, *Anolis gingivinus* **(41)** (see Anguilla) and *A. pogus*. *A. pogus* **(44)** is easily distinguishable from adult *A. gingivinus* by its size, which does not exceed 58 mm SVL (males), and from juvenile as well as adult *gingivinus* by its coloration, having a uniform light- to orange-brown dorsum. There is a turquoise-blue area around the eye, which may extend on to the upper head, while other parts of the head may be rust-brown in colour. The underside is dirty white, sometimes with a yellow tint. The dewlap is also white, with a lemon-yellow cast. The dewlap scales may be pale blue, blue-grey or white. Females are similar though duller but have a pale mid-dorsal stripe, which may be bordered by a darker stripe, and they may also have a white flank stripe. Unlike other islands, which have two coexisting species of anole, the two species do not have completely overlapping distributions. The larger species, *A. gingivinus*, is much more common at lower altitudes (although it is also frequently seen at the highest altitudes) while the smaller *A. pogus* is rarely seen at low altitudes but is abundant in the moist forest at higher altitudes. It is thought that this distribution may result from the two species being closer in size than is normally observed when two anole species coexist sympatrically, the greater similarity leading to greater competition for resources. However, there are other differences between the species, with *A. pogus* being usually found in shady perches whereas *A. gingivinus* is often seen in more exposed perches. *A. pogus* males typically perch no higher than 60 cm above ground, while females and juveniles are more likely to be found on the ground. They show a peak of feeding activity around dusk, often continuing until it is too dark to see them without a torch. *A. gingivinus* may perch quite high, and becomes noticeably less active later in the day.

The skink *Mabuya bistriata* **(20)** is present as well as *Iguana delicatissima* **(24, 25)** (see Dominica). There is one species of snake, the colubrid *Alsophis rijersmai* (see Anguilla).

ST BARTHÉLEMY

Better known as St Barts or St Barth, this island is the smallest of the French West Indies. It has a number of satellite islands, including Île Fourchue, Île Fregate and Île Chevreau. The terrestrial chelonid, *Geochelone carbonaria* **(38)** is reported from this island together with the whistling frog *Eleutherodactylus johnstonei* **(40)** and *Eleutherodactylus martinicensis* **(13, 14)** (see Dominica). The latter appears to be a recent introduction, probably from Guadeloupe through trading activity, since the three known localities are close to hotel construction sites[18]. The hotel gardens, which now form its habitat, presumably supply lusher habitats than naturally exist on this island.

The ground lizard *A. plei* **(43)** (described in the Anguilla account) shows considerable inter-island variation. For example, they are greenish brown with greenish blue sides, heavily spotted with pale green to cream-coloured spots on the main island, while on Île Fourchue they are uniform reddish brown with little dorsal pattern, although the sides are spotted or barred. *Anolis gingivinus* **(41)** (see Anguilla) is the only anole present. Like the other islands of the

Anguilla Bank, there are two dwarf geckos *(S. macrolepis, S. sputator* **(42)**), one skink *(M. bistriata)* **(18c, 20)** and *Iguana delicatissima* **(24, 25)**. The latter are found on the main island but are no longer common on the offshore islands such as Île Fourchue which they share with wild goats and seabirds. The islands are largely treeless and arid, approaching 90 m in altitude despite their small size. Sea turtles may nest on the beaches of Anse de Colombier, Anse des Flamands and Corossol on the north-west side of the island, from April to August. It has one species of snake, the colubrid *Alsophis rijersmai* (see Anguilla).

SABA

The island of Saba is the top of a young volcanic cone and lacks any coastal plain. The arid-adapted vegetation of the lower slopes has been severely degraded by feral goats, and contains many introduced ornamental species now growing wild, such as oleander. The natural vegetation of mid-altitudes has also been altered considerably by agricultural activity. Although the island lacks any freshwater sources, and does not receive very heavy rainfall, its higher slopes are frequently cloaked in clouds, and as a result are clothed with cloud forest.

45. Juvenile common iguana, *Iguana iguana* (Surinam)

The only amphibian species on Saba is *Eleutherodactylus john-stonei* **(40)** (see Dominica). There is one endemic lizard, *Anolis sabanus* **(46)**, which is common all over the island, although becoming less so towards the top of Mount Scenery, the highest point. These are medium sized lizards, reaching 69 mm SVL (males). Males have a pale ash-grey to tan background colour, heavily blotched with irregular dark patches that continue on to the head. The dewlap is pale yellow with a greenish to orange tint and the underside is pale greenish yellow to grey. Females are smaller, and are rather plain, the spots being reduced to mere smudges. They have a paler grey or olive-brown dorsal hue, and a mid-dorsal stripe, which may be plain or form a mottled ladder pattern.

The common or green iguana, *I. iguana* **(45)**, is the largest lizard in the Eastern Caribbean, with an SVL around 500 mm, with a much longer tail. Males reach larger sizes than females, and have larger heads, longer spines on the dorsal crest and larger femoral pores. Females and younger individuals are bright to dull green, while large males tend to be grey, although breeding males may be brighter in colour. The head may have a bluish tinge, and the tail is usually banded with black. However, it is very variable in appearance and the only definitive feature distinguishing it from its sister species is the presence of a large circular subtympanic scale. It uses

46. Male Saban anole, *Anolis sabanus* (Saba)

a variety of habitats and has been reported from mangroves and manchineel woodland (on other islands), and is often found in close association with human habitation. In Saba they can often be seen from the road, while their nesting burrows (resembling rabbit burrows) can be seen along the trail to Old Booby Hill[34]. Mating takes place during the dry season, and eggs are laid in warm, moist soil and hatch at the beginning of the wet season when new leaves as well as abundant insects are available for the young. Other than man and his domestic animals, the broad-winged hawk, *Buteo platypterus,* is likely to be its main predator.

Geckos include the widespread house gecko *Hemidactylus mabouia* **(36, 37)** and the dwarf gecko *S. sabanus* **(47)**. The latter is also found on other islands of the St Kitts Bank, and is a moderate-sized dwarf gecko, both sexes reaching just under 30 mm SVL. The dorsal ground colour varies from light to dark brown, with the head being more orange and striped with dark or dark-bordered lines extending from the tip of the snout. These may be broken up into spots or vermiculations. There is a dark, or dark-bordered, occipital spot and a dorsolateral row of paler spots on the trunk, although an occasional adult may be uniform brown. The ventral surface varies from white to light brown, and the throat is white or yellowish. The iris is brown. Females have a similar pattern to males, and juveniles differ only in having more pronounced longitudinal stripes. There is only one species of snake, the red-bellied racer *Alsophis rufiventris* **(48)**. It is a similar size to the Dominican *Alsophis* (see Dominica). Males have diffuse black-bordered brown

47. Dwarf gecko, *Sphaerodactylus sabanus* (St Kitts)

48. Male red-bellied racer, *Alsophis rufiventris* (Saba)

blotches which change into a diffuse dark mid-dorsal stripe posteriorly, while females have a paramedian series of streaks and smudges which become less obvious posteriorly. This species is widespread and fairly common in Saba, frequently being seen basking along trails and roadsides, and is also reported from St Eustatius. It appears to sunbathe and actively forages for lizards.

ST EUSTATIUS

The island, commonly referred to as Statia, has a distinctive profile, with a flat central area rising to hills that drop directly into the sea at the northern end, and the crater of a volcano known as the Quill at the southern end. The Boven National Park, recently established in the arid northern hills, is the best place to view *Iguana delicatissima* **(24, 25)**, while the rain forested crater of the Quill National Park provides an opportunity to see a variety of Statia's frogs, lizards and snakes. The ground lizard, *Ameiva erythrocephala,* is common on the route leading to the crater.

The fauna is very similar to other islands of the St Kitts Bank. The terrestrial chelonid, *Geochelone carbonaria* **(38)**, may possibly occur on this island, as may the whistling frog *Eleutherodactylus johnstonei* **(40)** (see Dominica). There is only one species of snake, the red-bellied racer *Alsophis rufiventris* **(48)** (see Saba). *Ameiva erythrocephala* is a moderately sized species, reaching 135 mm SVL (males). Sexes are similar in appearance, with a dark olive-green dorsal colour, tinged with russet. The head is lighter and more reddish, and the sides are rosy in colour. There are narrow stripes on the back and sides that run the length of the body but fade towards

49. Male anole, *Anolis bimaculatus* (Nevis)

50. Female anole, *Anolis bimaculatus* (Nevis)

the tail. The flanks are spotted and marbled with lighter markings. The underside of the body is blue-grey, while the throat and chin are flesh-coloured, and there is a darker area in between. Other lizards include *Anolis bimaculatus* **(49, 50)** and *A. schwartzi* (see St Kitts), *Hemidactylus mabouia* **(36, 37)**, *Iguana delicatissima* **(24, 25)** (see Dominica), *Sphaerodactylus sabanus* **(47)** (see Saba), *S. sputator* **(42)** (see Anguilla) and *Thecadactylus rapicauda* **(21, 22)** (see Dominica).

ST KITTS AND NEVIS

St Kitts and Nevis are not only part of the same political unit, but are also geologically very close, being separated by a 3.2-km (2-mile)-wide strait that is only 15 m (60 feet) deep at its deepest point. Their fauna is therefore very similar and will be described together. Both islands have substantially altered coastal vegetation, as a result of extensive establishment of plantations in the colonial era and of overgrazing by feral donkeys and goats and introduced white-tailed deer and green vervet monkeys. However, at higher elevations (above *c*. 300 m) on the volcanic cones, there are still substantial areas of rain forest and cloud forest.

Both islands have two amphibians, the widespread whistling frog *E. johnstonei* **(40)** (see Dominica) and the introduced marine toad, *Bufo marinus* **(51)**. The latter is a very large toad (up to 23 cm SVL in females, weighing over 1.5 kg) with pronounced parotoid glands. As its name suggests, it is tolerant of brackish conditions. In females and juvenile males the dorsal surface has irregular brown markings while adult males tend to be more uniformly coloured. The mating call is a low-pitched trill[35] that has been described as resembling a machine-gun or outboard motor, and is mainly heard from the end of the dry season through the height of the wet season. This species is widespread in Central and South America and has been introduced into this and other Lesser Antillean islands. There is a high population turnover each year and most specimens are young and much smaller than the maximum SVL. Adults and tadpoles have a high temperature tolerance but in the Lesser Antilles dehydration is thought to be a major cause of mortality. Nevertheless, they can reach high densities in some areas, having a rapid growth rate, early maturation and several breeding cycles per year. They can be found in a variety of habitats, but are especially abundant in disturbed and

51. Marine toad, *Bufo marinus* (Brazil)

open areas, and are frequently seen in close proximity to the sea. They feed primarily on ants and beetles but will take a wide variety of food including small vertebrates. They may lay eggs in small, temporary accumulations of water (e.g. in cavities in fallen trees), especially in the wet season although they may also breed in the dry season in more permanent bodies of water.

The presence of the tortoise *Geochelone carbonaria* **(38)** in St Kitts has not been verified; it is not present on Nevis. Lizard species present include the geckos *Hemidactylus mabouia* **(36, 37)** (not recorded in Nevis), *Thecadactylus rapicauda* **(21, 22)** (see Dominica), *Sphaerodactylus sabanus* **(47)** (see Saba) and *S. sputator* **(42)** (see Anguilla). The ground lizard, *Ameiva erythrocephala*, is scarce.

There are two species of *Anolis, A. bimaculatus* **(49, 50)** and *A. schwartzi*. Unlike the situation in St Martin, these two lizards differ quite considerably in size, as well as in other aspects of their ecology and behaviour, and occupy the same habitats throughout the island. *A. bimaculatus* reaches a large size (123 mm SVL in males) and large males are strikingly beautiful, with a bright grass-green or yellow-green dorsal ground colour, usually marbled or spotted with grey, brown or black on the trunk. The head and anterior trunk are bright turquoise, contrasting with the yellow-green or grey region around the eye. Ventral surfaces may be dull white, yellow or light green, and the dewlap is yellow or orange, sometimes contrasting with whitish scales. It is quite small relative to the size of the species. Females and smaller males are similar but less strikingly coloured.

They are relatively common and widely distributed throughout the island up to *c*. 300 m, and may be readily seen in large numbers around human habitations where suitable cover is available (for example, the grounds of the Montpelier Plantation Inn in Nevis). *A. schwartzi* is also common and widespread, although it occupies shadier habitats than its larger relative and so may be more localised. Some scientists consider this to be a subspecies of *A. wattsi* **(52)** (Antigua), together with *A. forresti* (Barbuda) and *A. pogus* **(44)** (St Martin). Whatever the exact species status, these are all clearly closely related and are very similar in appearance and habits.

St Kitts and Nevis also have two recorded species of snake, the colubrid *Alsophis rufiventris* **(48)** (see Saba) and the worm snake *Typhlops monastus* **(53)**. The latter has a trunk length of up to 258 mm and a tail length up to 44 mm, a dorsal surface of mid-brown and a lighter ventral surface. The subspecies from St Kitts and Nevis is also found on Barbuda and Antigua (including Great Bird Island), with another subspecies being found on Montserrat. As with other worm snakes it is insectivorous and fossorial, being found in soil or under rocks, logs or decaying vegetation.

52. Female anole, *Anolis wattsi* (Antigua)

53. Blind snake, *Typhlops monastus* (Antigua)

BARBUDA

Politically allied with Antigua, Barbuda is very different. Most of the island is only a few metres above sea level, although the 'Highlands' in the east rise to 39 m (128 ft). Best known for its breeding colony of frigatebirds, it is very arid and scrubby, and inhabited largely by herds of feral goats and donkeys. Wild boar and white-tailed deer have also been introduced and may have had a negative impact on the reptile populations, perhaps contributing towards the extinction of the Lesser Antillean iguana, *I. delicatissima* **(24, 25)**, which is known to have been present here in the past.

The ground lizard *Ameiva griswoldi* **(54)** is relatively common. Also found on Antigua, the population on Barbuda is slightly different in appearance, being dark brown with irregular creamy-green blotches. The flanks are pale bluish green and tan, spotted with black spots and markings, and the ventral colour is grey, with some black on the chest.

Anolis lizards are unusually scarce, being much more abundant around human habitation than in the surrounding scrub. There are two species, the larger being *Anolis leachi* **(55)** and the smaller *A. forresti* (see St Kitts and Nevis). The arid conditions, however, are likely to suit the tortoise *Geochelone carbonaria* **(38)** extremely well, and evidence of its presence can be seen in the form of chance encounters with its bleached carapace lying among the scrub. In spite of the aridity of the island, the frog *Eleutherodactylus johnstonei* **(40)** (see Dominica) is known to have been present, both in historical time and in the distant past, as fossils of the species have been found. The

54. Ground lizard, *Ameiva griswoldi* (Antigua)

55. Male anole, *Anolis leachi* (Antigua)

dwarf gecko, *Sphaerodactylus elegantulus,* is common all over the island while the turnip-tailed gecko, *Thecadactylus rapicauda,* may be restricted to the proximity of human habitation. The parthenogenetic lizard, *Gymnophthalmus underwoodi* (see Dominica), has recently been added to the species list for Barbuda[36]. There is also one species of snake, the worm snake *Typhlops monastus* (see St Kitts).

ANTIGUA

Antigua is a diverse island, with some relatively high mountains and rolling plains. The highest point, Boggy Peak, reaches an altitude of 400 m (1319 ft), and is situated in the south-western corner of the island, which represents an area of younger volcanism. There is little natural vegetation remaining in the lowlands of Antigua, the best of this occurring on the undeveloped east coast of the island around Ayres Creek, Nonsuch Bay and Half Moon Bay. Protection since 1912 has allowed secondary moist evergreen woodland to regenerate at Wallings, and this has now been developed into a conservation area. It is well worth a visit, with trails offering views of the island as well as chances to encounter Antiguan reptiles and amphibians. There are many offshore islands, especially to the north-east of the main island. Great Bird Island will be a natural magnet for the keen herpetologist, as it is only here that the Antiguan racer (one of the rarest snakes in the world) may be seen. The island has been the focus of intensive conservation efforts (see Conservation), but is nevertheless a popular day-trip destination for tourists and is easily reached. Ground lizards and anoles are also common (and very tame) here. Hawksbill turtles nest from May to December on the beach at Pasture Bay, on the north side of Long Island.

The tortoise *Geochelone carbonaria* **(38)** is reported historically from the main island of Antigua, but it is not certain whether it still occurs there. There are two species of frogs: the tree frog, *Eleutherodactylus johnstonei* **(40)** (see Dominica), and the large marine toad, *Bufo marinus* **(51)** (see St Kitts). While *E. martinicensis* **(13, 14)** is sometimes listed as occurring on this island, this probably results from mistaken identification[15].

The ground lizard, *Ameiva griswoldi* **(54)**, is now common only on the offshore islands, while the endangered *Iguana delicatissima* **(24, 25)**, known to have been present on this island in the recent past, is now considered extinct (see Conservation). There are two species of *Anolis*, the large *A. leachi* **(55)** and the smaller *A. wattsi* **(52)**. They are common all over the main island, although inexplicably absent from some of the offshore islets[30]. They share space in a similar manner to the two-species communities on the St Kitts Bank (see St Kitts).

The ubiquitous house gecko *Hemidactylus mabouia* **(36, 37)** and turnip-tailed gecko *Thecadactylus rapicauda* **(21, 22)** are present, and a careful search of areas of deep litter will find the dwarf gecko *S. elegantulus* **(56)**. Turning over rotten logs, stones and similar cover may reveal the worm snake *Typhlops monastus* **(53)** (see St Kitts). However, there is one questionable record of another worm snake *Leptotyphlops tenella* from Antigua (this species is otherwise found in Trinidad and South America). This is a much smaller snake, reaching only 170 mm SVL, and is more colourful, with a yellow spot on the front of the head, yellow spots on the posterior upper lip scales and a yellow tail, whereas *T. monastus* lacks yellow markings. It also has a more curved snout, with the upper lip overhanging, whereas *T. monastus* has a rounded head. The other species of snake, the Antiguan racer *Alsophis antiguae* **(57)**, although once present on the main island itself, is now found only on tiny Great Bird Island and is one of the most endangered snakes in the world (see Conservation). Specimens may grow up to about

56. Dwarf gecko, *Sphaerodactylus elegantulus* (Antigua)

57. Antiguan racer, *Alsophis antiguae*, Great Bird Island (Antigua)

660 mm long and have lateral stripes on a paler brown background with brown blotches on the anterior part. It is diurnal and actively forages for lizards and mice.

REDONDA

Redonda is an uninhabited and inhospitable island, politically part of Antigua and Barbuda although physically closer to Montserrat and Nevis. Guano and phosphate mining have been carried out in the past, but the island's steep and rugged terrain and uninviting coastline deter visitors. It used to be possible to arrange day trips to this island from Montserrat, but this is unlikely to be the case any longer. The vegetation consists of sedges, grasses and cacti. Due to its isolation, however, it is home to several endemic species of lizard, including *Anolis nubilis* and *Ameiva atrata* **(58)**. Interestingly, *A. atrata* is also a melanistic species like *A. corvax* (Little Scrub Island, Anguilla) and *A. corvina* (Sombrero) which come from very similar small and barren islands. The Redonda anole is also dingy in appearance, being various shades of grey all over, although the region surrounding the eye may be slightly yellower. Females have a hint of striping on the back in the region of the hindlimbs, and a flank stripe. In the absence of trees on the island (there is reportedly only one), they spend most of their time on the ground, in the

58. Ground lizard, *Ameiva atrata* (Redonda)

shade of large rocks. A dwarf gecko has recently been recorded from this island, and is considered to be a new, endemic, species[17] but it has yet to be given a formal scientific name or description. The skink *Mabuya bistriata* is also reported to be present, but no snakes have been reported.

MONTSERRAT

No other island in the Lesser Antilles has changed as drastically as Montserrat in recent years, after the Soufrière Hills volcano in the south of the island began erupting on 18 July 1995. Further major eruptions have occurred since, and currently the southern two-thirds of the island is off-limits, the capital Plymouth having been abandoned. The northern, accessible region is the most arid part of the island, with large areas of cactus scrub and xeric woodland. Ash falls that cover the whole of the island occur on a regular basis, and acid rain (recorded in some parts of the island to be more than 1000 times more acid than normal) has severely affected the vegetation. The rain forests of Chance's Peak have been totally destroyed. The Centre Hills, now largely in the exclusion zone, are the sole remaining habitat for Montserrat's native moist forest flora and fauna, including the mountain chicken *Leptodactylus fallax* **(35)** (see Dominica). Being an amphibian with a permeable skin, it might be expected to be among the most severely affected species. The impact of the eruption on these remnant populations is being closely monitored by the Forestry Department and conservation organisations. The other amphibians present, the tiny whistling frog *Eleutherodactylus johnstonei* **(40)** and the introduced marine toad *Bufo marinus* **(51)**, are still abundant.

Another casualty of the eruption appears to be the endemic ground lizard *Ameiva pluvianotata*, which has declined markedly in abundance since the event[30]. This ground lizard is moderate sized, with a variable colour pattern. Males may have a reddish or greyish tan dorsal ground colour with black speckling and lighter marbling, but may be almost patternless with a dull green dorsal surface and a dark blue head. Blue-grey spots occur on the upper thighs and sides of the tail, while the ventral surface is dull grey. Females have a grey dorsum, liberally spotted (as are the sides, limbs and tail) with lighter spots, and the underside is bluish. The flanks are dull green and may have brown stripes.

Anolis lividus, the endemic anole, is not abundant in the northern part of the island (although this may be more to do with the heavily altered, agricultural, landscape than the volcano itself). They are very variable in appearance over the island. Males may be plain grass-green or yellow-green in colour, sometimes with some lighter blue speckling on the anterior part of the body, and a rust-red wash on the head and limbs, or they may be olive green to grey, heavily blotched with pale spots. The area around the eye is usually orange or red, and there is sometimes a blue wash on the tail and the lower jaw. In the extreme northern part of the island, males have prominent black spots on the neck. The dewlap is pale ochre. Females are duller and browner, and have a mid-dorsal stripe or ladder pattern and a light flank stripe. The eyelids are usually white or yellow in colour. In the extreme north, they have much lighter and wider stripes, making the contrast with the background colour more pronounced.

The status of another endemic lizard, *Diploglossus montisserrati*, is undetermined. It is only known from a single specimen, a male. This is surprising as it is a relatively large lizard, measuring 180 mm SVL and with well-developed limbs. However, other species of the genus in the Greater Antilles are secretive, nocturnal animals, often passing unnoticed even if relatively common. This specimen was collected at Woodlands Spring, on the western flank of the Centre Hills, and viable populations may persist there. It is a rather plain brown lizard, with some white speckling on the flanks, legs and sides of the tail, indistinct darker brown lines in the neck region and white upper lip scales, speckled with brown.

Other lizards reported from Montserrat include the house gecko *Hemidactylus mabouia* **(36, 37)**, turnip-tailed gecko *Thecadactylus rapicauda* **(21, 22)** (see Dominica), the dwarf gecko *Sphaerodactylus fantasticus* **(23, 64–67)** (see Guadeloupe and Dominica), the skink *Mabuya bistriata* **(20)** (see Dominica) and the common iguana *Iguana iguana* **(45)** (see Saba). The terrestrial chelonid, *Geochelone carbonaria* **(38)**, is also reported from this island.

Montserrat also has two species of snake, the worm snake *Typhlops monastus* **(53)** (see St Kitts), and the racer *Alsophis antillensis* **(11, 27)** (see Dominica) which is subspecifically endemic to Montserrat. On Montserrat, this colubrid has a broad black mid-dorsal stripe with a double alternating series of yellow spots, and yellow dorsolateral lines bordered by black. It is (or was before the recent volcanic activity) fairly widespread with more reports from the west of the island.

THE GUADELOUPE ARCHIPELAGO
(including Grande Terre, Basse Terre, La Désirade and Îles de la Petite Terre)

The Guadeloupe Archipelago consists of two large islands, Grande Terre and Basse Terre, and a number of offshore islands of varying sizes. The two main islands are very different, belonging to different periods of volcanic activity. The older island, Grande Terre, has been eroded and capped with limestone, so is relatively flat and arid (although a small area of karst topography in the south-western corner is hilly and slightly lusher). It has also been extensively degraded by agricultural activities and the vegetation is scrubby. Basse Terre is a complete contrast, although it is separated from Grande Terre by an extremely narrow channel, the Rivière Salée. It is a young island and is dominated by tall volcanoes, including the highest mountain in the Lesser Antilles, Soufrière, which reaches 1467 m (4841 ft). The high mountains trap the moisture, leading to very high rainfall and a lush, rain-forested interior. In fact, the island is very similar to Dominica, although there is a more extensive coastal plain on the windward side. Most of the interior of the island has been set aside as a national park, and many trails have been established, allowing access to most parts. It is even possible to drive to an elevation of 1035 m (3397 ft) on the flanks of Morne

Soufrière, experiencing beautiful rain forest and the transition into elfin woodland on the way. Good points at which to stop and explore include the picnic site near St Claude (for montane anoles), La Maison du Volcan at 900 m, and just beyond the car park at Savane à Mulets at 1035 m (for endemic frogs, and also montane anoles at the former). Other good access points to the rain forest include the Chutes du Carbet, on the eastern flank of Soufrière.

La Désirade, off the eastern tip of Grande Terre, is dry and arid, and is easily accessible by air and ferry. The manchineel woods on the western tip are an especially good spot for iguanas. Just south of the eastern tip of Grande Terre lie the small uninhabited islands of Îles de la Petite Terre. They are a popular destination for day-trippers, and are easily accessed. Low and covered with thorny scrub and poisonous manchineel thickets, they are a haven for reptiles. Lesser Antillean iguanas are so abundant even the most unobservant visitor can see them, but anoles and dwarf geckos are also abundant. These islands are currently being developed as a national park (see Conservation).

Guadeloupe has the most diverse amphibian fauna in the Lesser Antilles, with the introduced marine toad *B. marinus* **(51)** (see St Kitts) and four species of whistling frog. Two of these, *Eleuthero-dactylus johnstonei* **(40)** and *E. martinicensis* **(13, 14)** (see Dominica), are widespread in the Lesser Antilles and on the Guadeloupean islands (although the former is absent from La Désirade). *E. bar-lagnei* and *E. pinchoni* are endemic to the highlands of Basse Terre. *E. barlagnei* is of moderate size for a whistling frog (32 mm SVL in females) and is dark brown to black, rather uniform or with two paler chevrons. There is an interocular bar and a broad black crural crossbar, and no red in the groin or on the hindlimbs. The ventral surface is dark grey with white spots on the throat, the iris is grey-brown above and darker below, and the toes have webs extending to the discs. Its call is a series of four or more, trilled, descending notes. This species is found from 120 to 750 m, and tends to be aquatic in mountain streams. *E. pinchoni* is small (20 mm SVL in females) with a dark brown dorsal surface which has a variable pattern. This may include darker chevrons and red-brown dorsolateral lines. The ventral surface is orange overlaid with dark brown with the groin bright orange-red while the iris is golden. This species is found from 200 to around 1600 m and tends to be terrestrial. Its call is a faint series of 'tiks' with a single rising 'wheep'.

The semi-aquatic chelonids, *Pelusios subniger* and *Trachemys scripta,* have been introduced, the former from Africa and the latter from North America. *Pelusios subniger* has an unkeeled carapace up to 30 m long. The head and neck are grey without markings while the carapace is darker grey-brown and the plastron can be from yellow to black with symmetrical markings[5]. In Guadeloupe, it is reported only from Grande Terre and is found in still water and rivers. It may be heliothermic during the day and search for food on land during the night. *Trachemys scripta* is smaller with a carapace up to 17 cm long in males and 28 cm long in females with a flared and serrated posterior margin. The coloration is brown with yellow and black markings. It is found on both Basse Terre and Grande Terre in vegetated fresh water. It is omnivorous with an emphasis on herbivory in adults and carnivory in juveniles.

The endemic ground lizard *Ameiva cineracea*, known from collections made by the earliest European explorers, is sadly now extinct (see Conservation). Nevertheless, there is a healthy existing lizard fauna, with nine species recorded. Guadeloupe (specifically Basse Terre) is the only island where both species of iguana, *I. delicatissima* **(24, 25)** (see Dominica) and *I. iguana* **(45)** (see Saba), coexist. However, this may not be a stable situation (see Conservation). The common iguana is the most obvious, easily seen around Fort St Charles and the Botanic Garden in the capital Basse Terre. However, there is a population of the Lesser Antillean iguana that still persists in the southern part of Basse Terre, and specimens are sometimes seen dead on the road. However endangered they are on the main islands, they have a stronghold on La Désirade and Îles de la Petite Terre, where they are abundant.

The endemic anole *Anolis marmoratus* **(59–63)** is a very interesting animal. It is extremely variable in appearance and other characteristics, and this variation has a strong geographical component. The descriptions that follow are for males. Females are similar but duller, usually lacking bold markings and often with a mid-dorsal stripe or pattern, and also a flank stripe. Montane animals are large and deep grass-green **(59)**, and have a variable number of irregular black (sometimes bluish) spots on the neck and front part of the body. The underside and dewlap is deep yellow or yellow-green. The eyelids are white (south) or bright yellow (north). On the southern part of the Caribbean coast **(60)**, the dark patches become more prevalent, in some cases merging into reticulations, while fading in intensity, and the dorsal ground colour fades to an olive grey. On the northern coast **(61)**, the lizards are plain grass-green with a turquoise wash over the head, neck and tail. They also have a peculiar conical form to their body scales,

59. Male anole, *Anolis marmoratus* (Chutes du Carbet, Basse Terre, Guadeloupe). Anoles from other montane areas lack the orange markings

60. Male anole, *Anolis marmoratus* (Trois Rivières, Basse Terre, Guadeloupe)

61. Male anole, *Anolis marmoratus* (St Rose, Basse Terre, Guadeloupe)

62. Male anole, *Anolis marmoratus* (Capesterre, Basse Terre, Guadeloupe)

which makes them look almost furry. In the south-eastern corner of Basse Terre, around the town of Capesterre **(62)**, the most striking colour pattern can be found. Here the lizards have plain blue-green bodies, but the head and neck are liberally spotted with bright orange vermiculations. Other combinations of these colour patterns can also be found. In the south-western part of Grande Terre, and extending into Basse Terre, the lizards are bright green with a deep yellow underside and dewlap, and some turquoise blue around the eye. In the drier parts of Grande Terre, they are pale grey-green with brown heads, and a pale lime-green underside. On La Désirade **(63)**, they are pale greenish with a yellow underside, extending on to the sides, the dorsal surface being covered with

63. Male anole, *Anolis marmoratus* (La Désirade)

darker vermiculations and the orbital area being intense rust-red. On Îles de la Petite Terre, they are similar, but the dorsal colour is greyer, and the chin is suffused with blue-grey.

Aspects of the colour pattern show a strong relationship to ecological variation. For example, animals from lusher environments are more intensely green, while those from drier environments are paler with a more marbled and blotched pattern. This matches exactly what is seen in *A. oculatus* **(4–8, 10)** in Dominica (see Dominica chapter). Eleven subspecies have been described of which two are from Îles des Saintes. However, these do not appear to hold up under close scrutiny, and while investigation at the genetic level has revealed that there are considerable differences between anole populations within the archipelago, they do not appear to correspond to the subspecies (also see the Introduction). It is entirely possible that, following a thorough investigation of the species, more than one species will be found to be present. The results of this work are, however, not yet available.

This dramatic variability is not restricted to this species alone. The dwarf gecko *Sphaerodactylus fantasticus* **(23, 64–67)** also has a large number of described subspecies reflecting the variability in

64. Adult male dwarf gecko, *Sphaerodactylus fantasticus* (Bois Sergent, Basse Terre, Guadeloupe)

65. Female dwarf gecko, *Sphaerodactylus fantasticus* (Bois Sergent, Basse Terre, Guadeloupe)

66. Adult male dwarf gecko, *Sphaerodactylus fantasticus* (Terre de Haut, Îles des Saintes)

67. Female dwarf gecko, *Sphaerodactylus fantasticus* (Terre de Haut, Îles des Saintes)

colour pattern and other characters. One subspecies, found around the capital city of Basse Terre, appears very similar to the Dominican population **(23)** (see Dominica) and recent studies[37] have shown that they are genetically almost identical, and the latter is very likely to be a case of a recent natural colonisation or accidental introduction.

Two species of the microteiid *Gymnophthalmus* have been reported from Guadeloupe (only the main islands) – *G. underwoodi* and *G. pleei* **(18b, 19)**. These species are described in the Dominica chapter. Other lizards present include the introduced geckos *Hemidactylus mabouia* **(36, 37)** and *Thecadactylus rapicauda* **(21, 22)** and the skink *Mabuya bistriata* **(18c, 20)**.

There are three (or possibly four) species of snake in Guadeloupe: two worm snakes, *Typhlops dominicana* **(30)** and two colubrids, the racer *Alsophis antillensis* **(11, 27)** and the grove snake *Liophis juliae* **(28)**. These are all also present in Dominica, and the main account for these species is given in that chapter. Another worm snake, *Leptotyphlops bilineata* (see Martinique) may also be present, but the record is considered questionable. *Typhlops dominicana* is subspecifically endemic to Guadeloupe and is fairly widespread on this island, being found on both Grande Terre and Basse Terre. There are no records from the other islands. The racer *Alsophis antillensis* has a double alternating series of light blotches on a darker background anteriorly which becomes predominantly dark posteriorly. This is considered a different subspecies from that on Dominica, and is found on Grande Terre and Basse Terre. Similarly, there is a subspecies of *Liophis juliae* endemic to Guadeloupe where it has been reported from south-western Grande Terre.

ÎLES DES SAINTES

Îles des Saintes are a group of eight small islands, only two of which are currently inhabited (although the presence of ruins indicates that Îlet à Cabrit was also formerly inhabited). The remaining islands are small and not readily accessible. Although politically part of Guadeloupe, Îles des Saintes are separated by a deep-water channel and were formed independently abut 5–8 million years ago. They are all relatively low, arid islands, with manchineel woodland fringing the coasts. The higher points of the two main islands have better-developed vegetation.

The fauna is very similar to the smaller islands of the Guadeloupe Archipelago. The only amphibian present is *E. martinicensis* **(13, 14)**. There are no terrestrial chelonids. There are four species of lizard currently present. A fifth, *Iguana delicatissima* **(24, 25)**, is known to have been present in the recent past but now appears to be effectively extinct (see Conservation), possibly as a result of competition with its close relative, the common iguana **(45)**. The latter certainly

68. Male anole, *Anolis marmoratus* (Terre de Haut, Îles des Saintes)

69. Male anole, *Anolis marmoratus* (Terre de Bas, Îles des Saintes)

lives up to its name in Îles des Saintes, where it can be seen peacefully grazing in fields of Terre de Haut, alongside the sheep. In the right season, the bright green, newly emerged young can be seen on the roadsides. It is abundant on the smaller islands, where it lives in (and on) manchineel thickets, which are poisonous to man but not to iguanas, or indeed to dwarf geckos. The latter belong to the *S. fanstasticus* **(66, 67)** complex and live in the caustic leaf litter of coastal manchineel scrub on the five larger islands.

Anoles are superabundant, and although they are currently considered subspecies of *A. marmoratus* (with a different one on Terre de Bas to the other islands), genetic data indicate that they are distinct (see Guadeloupe). Adult males on Terre de Haut **(68)** and smaller islands are greyish or greenish brown, with yellow suffusions laterally and on the head (on the nape and around the eye) and tail. The dewlap is yellow. Females are duller, with a mid-dorsal pattern and faint flank stripe. Males from Terre de Bas **(69)** are pale green, brighter towards the rear, and a lime-green underside (washed with yellow on the abdomen). However, the nape and back of the head are covered with fine grey vermiculations, and there is a pale flank stripe. The area around the eye is cream-coloured. The females are quite similar to the other islands, although the flank stripe is set off by dark speckling above and below. Their habits are very similar to other solitary anoles (see Dominica). The skink, *M. bistriata* **(18c, 20)** (see Dominica), is also present.

70. Grove snake, *Liophis juliae* (Terre de Haut, Îles des Saintes)

The racer *Alsophis antillensis* **(11, 27)** (see Dominica) is common and can often be seen around Fort Napoleon on Terre de Haut. While not reported in the literature, the grove snake *L. juliae* has also been found on Terre de Bas[38] **(70)**. The subspecies of *Alsophis antillensis* endemic to Terre de Bas has a beige to yellow-orange background with irregular black dorsolateral lines and transverse blotches, with the posterior of the body being black. There is another subspecies endemic to Terre de Haut, which has a bronze background with a dark vertebral stripe.

MARIE GALANTE

Politically part of Guadeloupe, this island is geologically distinct, being separated by deep-sea channels. It is low and limestone capped, resembling Grande Terre and reaching a maximum elevation of only 150 m in the eastern escarpment. It has been considerably altered by agricultural activities, and the vegetation is mainly secondary scrub.

Two species of whistling frog, *Eleutherodactylus johnstonei* **(40)** and *E. martinicensis* **(13, 14)**, are present. There are no native chelonids, but the semi-aquatic *Trachemys stejnegeri* has been introduced, probably from the Greater Antilles. The carapace is up to 21 cm long in males and up to 28 cm long in females. The skin of the head and neck is grey, brown or green with black-bordered yellow stripes and a dark red supra-temporal stripe. It inhabits fresh water and is heliothermic and omnivorous.

The Lesser Antillean iguana **(24, 25)** is known to have inhabited this island in the past, but is now extinct (see Conservation). The widespread skink *Mabuya bistriata* **(18c, 20)** is present, and the dwarf gecko presently ascribed to *S. fantasticus* (see Guadeloupe). The most interesting reptile here is the endemic *Anolis ferreus* **(71)**. The dorsal ground colour is yellow-green, with a blue-grey head with a yellowish orbital area. The males have very prominent tail crests. This species is unusually large for a solitary anole, with males reaching a maximum SVL of 119 mm. However, females only reach 65 mm, resulting in a huge difference in size between the sexes. Like the larger species of two-species islands, the lizards are primarily active during the middle of the day, and towards late afternoon retreat to high perches. This is in contrast to the typical

71. Male anole, *Anolis ferreus*
(Marie Galante)

behaviour of solitary anoles such as *Anolis oculatus* (Dominica) or
A. marmoratus (Guadeloupe) which often have a peak of activity at
dusk, during which they frequently forage on the ground. These
factors have led to suggestions that there may have been another
species of anole present at one time, which is now extinct.
However, there is no hard evidence to support this.

The island has two colubrids, *Alsophis antillensis* **(11, 27)** (see
Dominica and Guadeloupe) and *Liophis juliae* **(28)** (see Dominica),
which is subspecifically endemic to Marie Galante.

DOMINICA

There is a detailed description of Dominica on pages 20–51.

MARTINIQUE

Martinique is the largest island in the Eastern Caribbean. It has a
complex geological history, having erupted at different periods, so
that the southern part of the island is considerably older than the
northern part. In addition, it was at one time at least three distinct
islands, before relatively recent (on a geological timescale) volcanic

activity joined them together. This diversity of origin is clearly visible in the landscape, with rugged volcanoes towards the north, clothed in thick rain forest, while there are rounded hills in the central area with xeric woodland, which gives way to the much flatter and extremely arid southern end (especially the south-eastern peninsula). There are several protected areas, for example the Donis Arboretum along the Route de la Trace (rain forest) and the Caravelle peninsula (littoral forest), which make good spots for reptile watching. Care should be taken as the island is home to a venomous snake, although the chances of encountering one are not high.

There are four species of amphibian on this island. Two are whistling frogs, *E. johnstonei* **(40)** and *E. martinicensis* **(13, 14)** (see Dominica). The marine toad *Bufo marinus* **(51)** is also present. The fourth species, *Colostethus chalcopis*[4], was only discovered in 1990 by biologists working on the flanks of Morne Pelée near sunset, who heard an unidentifiable call. It was a remarkable find as it is the only species of this family known from Caribbean islands (although two species also occur on Trinidad). It is a small species (females grow to 18 mm SVL), and the juveniles may be confused with other species, but can be distinguished by the presence of digital scutes and a more elongated head shape. In adults, the belly is uniform pale orange, and males also have a black throat collar. The dorsum is light brown with darker brown markings, and the upper part of the iris is coppery (lower part brown). It lives in ravines in montane rain forest, at elevations of around 500 m, and at higher elevations in elfin woodland. It is active at dawn and dusk (crepuscular), at which times there are peaks in calling, especially at dusk. The call consists of a single note. It is not surprising that it escaped notice for so long, since it is extremely secretive in behaviour, retreating under leaves and rocks at the slightest disturbance. Clutches of around three eggs are laid and tadpoles are non-feeding.

This island was once home to two endemic species of lizard, the teiid *Ameiva major* and the iguanid *Leiocephalus herminieri*. These are now known only from museum specimens collected by the early European explorers. Populations of the endangered *Iguana delicatissima* **(24, 25)** (see Dominica chapter) are, however, still present.

Like the other large and climatically diverse islands of the Lesser Antilles, the endemic anole (*Anolis roquet)* shows considerable variation in morphological characteristics which, once again, is reflected in a large number of named subspecies **(72, 73)**. Although

72. Copulating pair of montane anoles, *Anolis roquet* (Trace Jesuits, Martinique). The male is larger

73. Male anole, *Anolis* sp. (southern tip of Martinique)

this species is also variable in body size, shape and scalation[39], only colour pattern variation (primarily of adult males) is described here. The dorsal ground colour may be green, grey-green, brown, or grey-brown, and some populations also have areas of turquoise blue. There are a variety of dark markings, including marbling, spots and chevrons, as well as a variety of light markings, including a flank stripe. Both the ventral and dewlap colours are highly variable. The addition of information from genetic studies has indicated that while some of this morphological variation seems to result from within-species local adaptation, more than one species may be present on the island. This anole is capable of making a squeaking noise when caught.

Other lizards present include the microteiid *Gymnophthalmus pleei* **(18b, 19)** (see Dominica chapter) and the geckos *Hemidactylus mabouia* **(36, 37)**, *Thecadactylus rapicauda* **(21, 22)** and *Sphaerodactylus vincenti* **(34)**. The latter, while also found on neighbouring islands, is extremely diverse within Martinique, reflected by the naming of six subspecies on this island alone (however, note that no detailed genetic analysis has yet been done of this species). Although in some populations there is sexual dichromatism, most specimens have either a pair of black-edged white ocelli or a light nuchal bar (which may be slightly V-shaped), and the dorsal ground colour is usually some shade of brown, often speckled with darker brown. There may be light lines extending from above and behind the eyes to the level of the ocelli, where they may fuse or extend further on to the trunk. The limbs may also be marbled with darker pigment, and the tail is usually adorned with dark-edged white spots or crossbars. The colour of the iris, throat and belly is very variable. It is found all over the island, in a wide range of vegetation types and climatic zones, wherever there is enough ground debris to retain moisture. It is a large species, with both sexes reaching 40 mm. Females reach sexual maturity at about 25–26 mm SVL (which is achieved in about 19–20 months), and produce eggs at regular intervals. Incubation takes about two months.

Martinique currently has only two species of snake: the worm snake, *Leptotyphlops bilineata* and the pit viper, *Bothrops lanceolata*. No colubrid snakes remain on the island today. The worm snake is a small snake (trunk up to 108 mm) with a short blunt snout and a uniform coloured mid-dorsal surface with light dorsolateral lines on dark sides and a light ventral surface. This cryptic fossorial snake may be widespread in Martinique and is also reported from St Lucia, Barbados and Guadeloupe (although the latter is questionable). The pit viper is large, growing up to 1.5 m long. It has a dark, clearly defined, temporal stripe and a dorsal pattern of dark, broad U-shaped markings on a grey-brown background. It is endemic to Martinique, and although relatively widespread, is confined to wetter regions and is not seen very frequently. Young are found from July to October with up to 75 young in a litter. Snakebites have been recorded for over three centuries, but fatalities are now rare.

ST LUCIA

St Lucia, like Martinique, is also made up of several parts of different ages. The northern part is geologically older, as is reflected by its lower, more rolling topography and drier climate. The central mountain range, by contrast, is young and lofty (with peaks exceeding 900 m) and clothed in rain forest. The drier coastal slopes of this range have extensive areas of xeric woodland. There are a number of offshore islets off the east coast, and the two tiny Maria islands off the southern tip of the island are now managed as a nature reserve, having assumed great significance as the last refuge for some of St Lucia's endemic reptiles (see below and Conservation). It is possible to visit Maria Major by special arrangement, although the Forestry Department tries to regulate the number of visitors to protect the delicate ecosystem of this small island. The island is clothed with white cedar and birch gum thickets, which give way to cactus scrub on the more exposed slopes. Other areas of interest include the Union Nature Trail near the offices of the Forestry Department, which affords the opportunity to observe the reptiles of the dry forest, as well as a chance to see the large male green iguana in the mini-zoo at the same site. The area around Grande Anse is said to be densely populated with pit vipers, although the authors searched for hours before turning up a small specimen in a dry riverbed. Sea turtles nest on the undeveloped beaches of the north-east coast from February to October.

Three species of amphibian, the whistling frog E. johnstonei **(40)** (see Dominica chapter), the introduced marine toad, B. marinus **(51)** (see St Kitts) and Scinax rubra (see St Martin) are recorded from St Lucia. They are widely distributed over the island, although the latter two will be primarily found in disturbed and agricultural areas.

74. Male anole, *Anolis luciae* (St Lucia)

Unusually, there are three species of anole on this island. Two of these, *Anolis extremus* (see Barbados) and *Anolis wattsi* **(52)** (see Antigua), have been introduced from other islands, and have a very restricted range in St Lucia, being found only in the environs of the capital Castries. There is only one species of native anole, *Anolis luciae* **(74)**, which is endemic. While it varies in appearance over the island, this is not as dramatic as the species on the three islands to the north and no subspecies have been described. It is widely distributed over the island and its offshore islets and the dorsal ground colour varies from brown in the drier parts of the island to apple green in the wetter parts. Some populations have blue tints on the sides, and the ventral surface may be whitish or with a yellow tinge. There may be reticulations or chevron patterns on the dorsal surface, or it may be patternless. The dewlap and iris are also variable in colour, and the region around the eye may be white, blue or greenish. Females are similar to males but duller, and they may have a mid-dorsal stripe or dark chevrons. They are similar in their habits to other solitary anoles, and appear to be resisting displacement by the introduced species (see Conservation).

The common iguana is recorded from St Lucia, but it has very infrequently been encountered in the wild in recent years[40], and may not be established on the island. Other common and widespread lizards include the cryptic microteiid *Gymnophthalmus pleei* **(18b, 19)** and the geckos *Hemidactylus mabouia* **(36, 37)** and *Thecadactylus rapicauda* **(21, 22)**. There are two species of dwarf gecko, *Sphaerodactylus microlepis* **(75)** and *S. vincenti* **(34)** (see Martinique). The former is endemic to St Lucia (although a single specimen reported to be from Dominica exists; see Dominica). It is smaller than *S. vincenti*, both

75. *Sphaerodactylus microlepis* (St Lucia)

sexes reaching 34 mm SVL. There is no sexual dimorphism, but the colour pattern is variable. There is usually a series of six or seven dark crossbands between the limbs, against a light brown or grey background. However, these may fade in some adults until they are indistinguishable from the background. The tail is vivid coral to pale orange, with ladder-shaped markings. The underside is white to yellow, and the chin is marked with dark stripes extending to throat or chest. The top of the head is light brown or yellow, with a darker pattern and dark stripes extending from behind the eye and joining behind the neck.

Many of St Lucia's original reptile species have been extirpated from the main island, and now only persist on offshore islands (see Conservation). This includes the St Lucia whiptail, *Cnemidophorus vanzoi* **(76)**, now found only on Maria Major **(77)**. The only

76. Male ground lizard, *Cnemidophorus vanzoi* (Maria Major Islet, St Lucia)

77. Maria Major Islet, St Lucia

representative of the genus in the West Indies, it resembles and behaves like the *Ameiva* ground lizards of other islands, actively foraging for invertebrates during the middle of the day, and retreating to burrows at cooler times of day. Also restricted to the offshore islands of Maria Major and Dennery Island is another species of *Hemidactylus, H. palaichthus*. This can be distinguished from its congener by its more spiny appearance and lamellae that extend right to the base of the fourth and fifth toes. A lowland endemic species in northern South America, it seems to be restricted to offshore rocks and islands in the Lesser Antilles (other reports are from Trinidad and Tobago[6]), possibly due to the absence of predators or competitors. It is primarily nocturnal but can be seen hiding in rock crevices during the day.

There are five species of snake known from St Lucia: the worm snake, *Leptotyphlops bilineata* (see Martinique); the boa, *B. constrictor* **(3)**; the pit viper, *Bothrops caribbaea* **(78)**; and the colubrids, *Clelia errabunda* and *Liophis ornatus* **(79)**. The subspecifically endemic St Lucian boa constrictor is widespread, but less frequently encountered than the species is on Dominica, and may be more vulnerable to extinction. A breeding ball consisting of one large female and five smaller males **(3)** was encountered by the authors in February 1995 in the Roseau river valley.

The St Lucian pit viper, *Bothrops caribbaea* **(78)**, is reported to grow to 1300 mm, but much larger specimens are possible. It has a grey to grey-brown background with grey to brown markings which are clear mid-dorsally but less distinct laterally. The temporal stripe is irregular. This venomous species is endemic to St Lucia where it is reported to have a lowland distribution and can be readily found along river valleys. During a recent tropical storm, which was accompanied by torrential rain, local fishermen reported finding these snakes some way out to sea, presumably washed out by floods[40]. It is terrestrial or semi-arboreal and is known to feed on rodents, but is likely to take a much broader spectrum of food.

The colubrid *Clelia errabunda*[23] is now only known from museum specimens. Originally thought to belong to the species *C. clelia*, it has been shown to be a distinct species endemic to St Lucia. Other species of the genus *Clelia* are known to be specialist feeders on venomous snakes, and this can be confirmed to have been the case for this extinct species, as one museum specimen was preserved in the act of swallowing a large *Bothrops*. It is ironic that this natural predator of *Bothrops* was probably helped to extinction by the huge pressure put upon it by the bounty on snakes offered in an attempt to eradicate the venomous snake.

78. Pit viper, *Bothrops caribbaea* (St Lucia)

79. St Lucian grove snake, *Liophis ornatus* (Maria Major Islet, St Lucia)

The other colubrid, *Liophis ornatus* **(79)**, can grow up to 1235 mm. It may have alternating yellow and diagonal spots forming streaks towards the posterior or have a broad brown stripe on the dorsum. It is probably extinct on St Lucia itself, but until recently was found on Maria Major. However, sightings are so infrequent and the island so small that it is not certain that this species is safe from extinction and it is, perhaps, the most endangered snake species in the world (see Conservation). Based on knowledge of the habits of other snakes of the genus, it is possible to guess that it probably actively forages for lizards during the day.

BARBADOS

Barbados is largely flat, and has been under intensive cultivation for more than 300 years, leaving little natural vegetation. Some examples of remnants of natural vegetation include evergreen and semi-deciduous seasonal woodland in Turner's Hall Wood, seasonal forest in Hackleton Undercliff Woods, xeric woodland at Bath and cactus scrub in the Scotland district[41]. Over the larger part of the island, reptiles may now be restricted largely to the hedgerows surrounding sugarcane fields, or to wooded gullies.

Two amphibians are found on the island: the small whistling tree frog, *Eleutherodactylus johnstonei* **(40)**, and the large terrestrial marine toad, *Bufo marinus* **(51)**. The latter species has been introduced on to the island by man, as probably has the tortoise *Geochelone carbonaria* **(38)** (albeit much longer ago). Other lizard species include *Gymnophthalmus underwoodi*, *Hemidactylus mabouia* **(36, 37)** and *Mabuya bistriata* **(18c, 20)** (all described in the Dominica chapter).

Barbados does not lack its share of endemic species, however. The tree lizard, *Anolis extremus*, is one of these (although it is now found in other islands as well, having been introduced by man). It has adapted well to the presence of man, and is ubiquitous and abundant all over the island. The dorsal ground colour is mossy green, heavily marked on the anterior of the trunk with dark markings, sometimes with white spots superimposed. The head is blue-grey to lavender, with blue eyelids, and the belly is yellow. The females are smaller, duller, and may have a mid-dorsal stripe.

Another endemic, the ground lizard *Kentropyx borckiana*, is the only member of this genus in the Eastern Caribbean (the Trinidad population formerly assigned to this species has since been shown to belong to another species[6]). It grows to 100 mm SVL, and has a cylindrical body with well-developed limbs, with a greyish to pinkish-brown upper surface with lighter dorsolateral stripes bordered by darker bands. The head and neck are greenish, and the body is chestnut brown on the sides. The underside of the body is pinkish, and that of the head whitish. Not much is known about its habits, as it is very rare. A sighting in 1988 confirms that it probably still exists on Barbados, in the deep wooded gullies that are probably a refuge for more than one species of reptile on this intensively farmed island. However, the status of another endemic lizard, the gecko *Phyllodactylus pulcher*, is undetermined. Nothing is known about its habits, although it is presumably nocturnal, arboreal and insectivorous. It has a maximum SVL of 62 mm and is cream coloured. The dorsum is mottled with brown, or banded with broad brown crossbands or with longitudinal brown lines. There is also a dark line extending through the eye from the nostril to the shoulder region.

Barbados has a worm snake, *Leptotyphlops bilineata* (see Martinique), and an endemic colubrid, *Liophis perfuscus*. The colubrid, *L. perfuscus*, grows to about 800 mm and is brown to dark brown dorsally and paler laterally with light lateral stripes to the rear. This species is endemic to Barbados where it is likely to have lived in mesic habitats and probably actively foraged for lizards and frogs during the day. However, it is almost certainly extinct, not having been sighted for more than a hundred years. However, during surveys of the island to search for evidence of this species, herpetologists found another, previously unknown, species of colubrid. It has been identified as a new species of the genus *Mastigodryas*[30]. Regrettably, this species could be destined for extinction in the very near future, as the size of the habitat available to it seems too small to support a viable population.

ST VINCENT

St Vincent is composed entirely of volcanic peaks that rise steeply from the sea, and is dominated by the still active volcano, La Soufrière (1234 m), situated at its northern end. The south-west of the island, in the shelter of the mountains, is the driest part of the island. Kings Hill Forest Reserve, one of the earliest protected areas in the Caribbean, is an area of dry forest, while the Vermont Nature Trails, established to allow access to the habitat of the rare St Vincent parrot, also allow access to montane reptiles and amphibians.

The widespread whistling frog *E. johnstonei* **(40)** (see Dominica) and the marine toad *B. marinus* **(51)** (see St Kitts) occur on St Vincent. *Leptodactylus validus* **(80)** (formerly known as *L. wagneri*[6]) is also found on the Grenadines and Grenada. It is a fairly large frog (about 78 mm SVL) with a yellow-brown dorsal surface with dark brown or black markings. The ventral surface is bright yellow at the groin with grey stippling. Its call is a metallic high pitched rattle (oit oit oit)[33]. It is considered to be endemic to Trinidad and Tobago and has dispersed into the Lesser Antilles more recently[6]. It is a forest or forest edge species, which may occasionally venture into more human-influenced habitats. It eats crickets, beetles, ants and centipedes and reproduction takes place in the wet season, when it makes foam nests in temporary water bodies.

Another species of whistling frog, *Eleutherodactylus shrevei* **(81)**, is endemic to this small island. *E. shrevei* is a forest dweller, restricted to pristine montane forest[42]. There is evidence that its habitat has become more restricted recently. It may be seen together with *E. johnstonei* **(40)** on sparsely vegetated lava flows of

80. *Leptodactylus validus*
(formerly *L. wagneri*) (St Vincent)

81. *Eleutherodactylus shrevei*
(St Vincent)

Soufrière, but is absent from its lower slopes and coconut groves. It is also present at high altitudes (above *c.* 600 m) in the south of the island. It has a dark brown dorsum and a light brown underside. The lips are mottled, and the posterior part of the thighs is carmine red in colour. The upper iris is bronze (sometimes grey). Its call, being a series of clicks rather than whistles, is easily distinguishable from *E. johnstonei.* Males call from high perches, although they may call from terrestrial bromeliads in more barren areas where these provide the only perches. Calls begin before sunset. It is a very shy species, being easily disturbed by torchlight.

The tree lizards, *Anolis griseus* and *A. trinitatis,* are also endemic to St Vincent. They are distributed all over the island from sea level to an altitude of about 900 m. The latter (which has also been introduced on to Trinidad) is the smaller of the two, with males reaching 74 mm SVL. The dewlap is very large, extending well into the abdominal region. They are green to greenish blue above, with some blue stippling on the head and anterior trunk, with yellow on jaws and ventral regions and a dark region surrounding the eye. Females have smaller dewlaps and are duller. They usually perch low, below *c.* 3 m (10 ft). *A. griseus* is much larger, reaching 136 mm SVL. It usually perches high, but sometimes descends to the ground (especially females). The ground colour is mossy grey-brown, although there may also be yellow tinges on the face (including the orbital region) and the limbs. The belly is pale, greenish or yellowish grey, and the dewlap is dull orange (in both sexes). There are irregular darker markings on the body.

82. Ground lizard, *Ameiva ameiva* (Surinam)

Most of the other lizards present are found on other islands in the Lesser Antilles. They include the microteiid *Gymnophthalmus underwoodi*, the common iguana *Iguana iguana* **(45)** (see Saba) and the geckos *Sphaerodactylus vincenti* **(34)** (see Martinique), *Thecadactylus rapicauda* **(21, 22)** and *Hemidactylus mabouia* **(36, 37)** (see Dominica). The ground lizard *Ameiva ameiva* **(82)** is found elsewhere in the Lesser Antilles, as well as being widely distributed in tropical South America. It is a moderate-sized species reaching *c.* 150 mm SVL. While it is very variable in appearance, it usually has a pattern of light spots on a darker ground dorsally, with darker sides either dotted or with yellowish stripes. Its habits are similar to other ground lizards. However, this species (and the skink *M. bistriata*) may now be extinct on St Vincent.

St Vincent has two species of colubrid snake, *Mastigodryas bruesi* **(83)** and *Chironius vincenti*. *Mastigodryas bruesi* grows to about 830 mm long and has a blue-grey to brown background with light lateral stripes. There are records of this snake from the south-west of St Vincent where it lives in xeric habitats. It is also found on the Grenadines and Grenada. It is diurnal, feeding on frogs and lizards and is found both on the ground and in bushes (where it sleeps at night). The other colubrid on St Vincent, *Chironius vincenti*, grows to over a metre in length and has a uniform slate black colour with paler colour around the mouth and ventral surface. This species is

83. *Mastigodryas bruesi* (Bequia)

84. Tree boa, *Corallus hortulanus* (Surinam)

85. Tree boa, *Corallus hortulanus* (Surinam)

endemic to St Vincent and is probably restricted to altitudes between 150 and 330 m. There is also a boid snake, *Corallus hortulanus* **(84, 85)**. This species reaches 1600 mm SVL, and in St Vincent is a grey snake with a darker rhombic pattern on the dorsal surface. It is found in a wide range of habitats, including mangrove swamps, xeric woodland and orchards, but is uncommon in rain forest. It is nocturnal, preying heavily on *Anolis* when smaller and rodents when larger. Birds and other lizards may also occasionally be taken. Females with up to 40 eggs have been recorded.

THE GRENADINES

This group of over three dozen small islands and cays have a very similar fauna to their larger neighbours, St Vincent in the north (with which, apart from the two southernmost islands, they are politically allied) and Grenada in the south (which is part of the same island bank). Although volcanic in origin, they are old and eroded, primarily arid, islands. Many of them have also suffered overgrazing by feral goats. The largest of the islands is Bequia. Union Island, one of the most densely populated, also has the islands' highest peak, 304 m high Mt Tabor. The island is covered with xeric woodland and patches of cactus scrub, with manchineel and seagrape fringing its coastline. Carriacou, politically allied with Grenada rather than the rest of the islands in the chain, is covered with cactus and acacia thorn scrub.

While the whistling frog *E. johnstonei* **(40)** (see Dominica) appears to be a recent, and perhaps human-mediated introduction to the Grenadines, *Leptodactylus validus* **(80)** (see St Vincent) is recorded from Bequia only. The tortoise *Geochelone carbonaria* **(38)** is present as are the geckos *Hemidactylus mabouia* **(36, 37)** and *Thecadactylus rapicauda* **(21, 22)**, the skink *Mabuya bistriata* **(18c, 20)** and the common iguana *I. iguana* **(45)**. The anole *Anolis aeneus*

(86) and the ground lizard *Ameiva ameiva* **(82)** (see St Vincent) are found throughout the islands (although the latter may appear very different on different islands). *Anolis richardii* **(87)** (see Grenada) is found on the larger islands of Carriacou and Bequia, and the microteiid *Bachia heteropa* (see Grenada) is recorded from Canouan and Bequia. *Gymnophthalmus underwoodi* has also been reported recently from Bequia[43], and there is an endemic species of dwarf gecko, *Sphaerodactylus kirbyi,* which was recently discovered on this island[44]. The latter appear to be closely related to *S. vincenti* **(34)** from St Vincent but differ from them in being smaller (up to 25 mm SVL) and stouter, with larger scales and less rich head coloration. They are sombre animals, being various shades of grey-brown above and below, with irregular small blotches on the body and faint stripes on the head. However, there may be a yellow wash on the chin, throat (which may be lightly marked with ashy streaks) and sides of the neck, and the underside of the tail is mottled with rosy orange. A slate-grey inverse V-shape extends from the region of the hindlimbs on to the base of the tail. They are not at all common, however.

The islands also have one species of colubrid, *Mastigodryas bruesi* **(83)** (see St Vincent) which is widespread and can occur in quite xeric habitats. The boid *Corallus hortulanus* **(84, 85)** (see St Vincent) is recorded from Bequia, Îsle de Quatre, Union, Carriacou and Petit Martinique. Bequia specimens resemble the St Vincent rather than the Grenadian population.

86. Male anole, *Anolis aeneus* (Bequia, Grenadines)

87. Male anole, *Anolis richardii* (Bequia, Grenadines)

GRENADA

Grenada is rugged and thickly forested, with its highest point (Mt St Catherine) reaching 840 m (2757 ft). Most of the island is volcanic, although there are some limestone areas in the north. The Grand Étang Forest Reserve, in the centre of the island, gives access to the habitat of the endemic whistling frog. On the north coast of the island, the coastal woodlands of the Levera National Park are home to common iguanas, and sea turtles nest on its fringing beaches. La Baye Rock, off the Atlantic coast, is covered with cactus and thorn scrub, and inhabited by iguanas as well as seabirds. Visits can be arranged with local fishermen.

The widespread whistling frog, *E. johnstonei* **(40)**, is also found in Grenada. Another species, *E. euphronides* **(88)** is an endemic, montane forest species apparently having become more restricted in distribution in recent years through displacement by *E. johnstonei*[42]. This might have resulted in the splitting of a formerly continuous population into two separate populations centred around Mt St Catherine and in the vicinity of Grand Étang Forest Reserve.

88. *Eleutherodactylus euphronides* (Grenada)

Males can be heard calling only around dusk, usually from high perches. Females are more usually encountered at or near ground level. This species has a dark brown dorsum and a cream underside, with mottled lips and a bronze-coloured upper iris. The posterior surfaces of the thigh are orange-brown, and there is a dark supra-tympanic stripe running from the corner of the eye to the armpit. *Leptodactylus validus* **(80)** (see St Vincent) is also present.

The tortoise *Geochelone carbonaria* **(38)** (see Dominica) is reported from this island, as are the ground lizard *Ameiva ameiva* **(82)** (see St Vincent), the geckos *Hemidactylus mabouia* **(36, 37)** and *Thecadactylus rapicauda* **(21, 22)**, the skink *Mabuya bistriata* **(18c, 20)** (see Dominica), and the common iguana *I. iguana* **(45)** (see Saba). Two species of tree lizard are present. *Anolis richardii* **(87)** is endemic to Grenada and the Grenadines, although it has been introduced to Tobago (where it is the only anole present). It is a 'giant' species, attaining a SVL of 140 mm (males). It is dark green or brown dorsally, and greenish grey to yellow below. Females and juveniles often have a yellow or cream lateral stripe. The dewlap (present in both sexes) may be orange, yellow or grey-green. Adults occupy the trunks of tree, but juveniles are more terrestrial. *A. aeneus* **(86)** is a medium sized species, males reaching 77 mm SVL (although it may not reach this size on more arid, less productive islands). The ground colour varies from pale ash grey, olive-green or chocolate, with a pattern of mottling or fine speckles that are more obvious on the darker backgrounds. The ventral surface is pale, often with darker mottling along the sides. The dewlap is white or dull green, with a contrasting yellow, orange or mustard-coloured spot near its front edge. Females are brown, with a mid-dorsal ladder or stripe and a light flank stripe. This species has been the focus of many studies of the complex behaviour and ecological strategies shown by *Anolis* lizards.

Also present is the microteiid *Bachia heteropa*, which has probably been introduced from Tobago[6]. It has a maximum SVL of 64 mm, and the tail may be more than 1.5 times as long. The limbs are very small relative to the body length, with a reduced number of digits (four on the forelimbs and two on the hindlimbs), giving it a worm-like appearance. The body is covered by rows of large, hexagonal, overlapping scales. This lizard is a leaf-litter-dwelling forest species, feeding on arthropods and their larvae.

Grenada is reported to have three (possibly four) species of colubrids, and one boid, *Mastigodryas bruesi* **(83)**, is recorded from the southern half of Grenada which is the southern extremity of its range (see St Vincent). *Clelia clelia* **(89)** is also found on Trinidad and the mainland. It is a large species, growing to almost 3 m SVL. Adults are usually uniformly blue-black above, with a whitish ventral surface. There may be white, cream or red on the lips. Juveniles, however, are brightly coloured, being red above with a black crown and a light collar. There is also some black pigmentation on the nape, posterior to the collar. It is a forest species, often found near water, and is mainly nocturnal in habits. It feeds almost exclusively on other reptiles, including venomous snakes, but some mammals have been recorded in its diet. It lays 16–20 eggs per clutch. *Pseudoboa neuwiedi* grows to about 900 mm, the juveniles being pink to orange with the top of the head being brown or black with a creamy yellow collar behind the parietals. The adults tend to have a uniform red, pink or grey-brown dorsum with a darker head

89. Juvenile *Clelia clelia* (Surinam)

and lighter ventral surface. This genus appears superficially similar to *Clelia* to which it is related, and can be distinguished by having single subcaudals (paired in *Clelia*) and a unique spade-shaped rostral scale. The species may be extinct in Grenada, but is found in Central and South America. It is a crepuscular, or nocturnal, terrestrial snake which inhabits mesic habitats such as forests and feeds on reptiles (including members of its own species) and small mammals – three to nine eggs are laid. *Liophis melanotus* grows to about 430 mm long with a light yellow or pinkish background and a wide dark vertebral stripe. It is also found in Trinidad, Tobago and northern South America. It is an actively foraging diurnal terrestrial snake, which may eat fish, amphibians and lizards. Grenadian specimens of the boid *Corallus hortulanus* **(84, 85)** (see St Vincent) are more variable and colourful than those from St Vincent. They may be pale yellow in colour, immaculate or flecked with brown. Other specimens may be rose or rust-red, with dark ovoid markings, or pale grey with rhombic, or occasionally chevronate, markings. There is also a species of *Typhlops, T. tasymicris*. Not much is known about its habits, which are likely to be similar to those of other species. Reaching a total of 180 mm, it is bicoloured, with an unpigmented venter and the dorsal surface appears to have light lines.

Conservation

Conservation threats to reptiles and amphibians in the Lesser Antilles (and other islands) are a result of the features of their ecosystems, which render them vulnerable to perturbation. Typically, they have few species and relatively few predators. The lack of native predators may render endemic species very vulnerable to introduced predators such as the mongoose, and the lack of closely related competitors may render them vulnerable to replacement or genetic introgression from introduced, closely related, competitors, e.g. whistling frogs, anoles and iguanas introduced between islands. On the other hand, because small islands have fewer species, some individual species, e.g. some anoles, may occur in large numbers across a wide range of habitats, which renders them less vulnerable. The Lesser Antilles offer examples of extremes of both endangered individual species (they have the two most endangered snakes in the world) and endangered habitats.

EXTINCTIONS

It is difficult to know the full extent of extinctions that have already occurred because of the difficulty of knowing historical distributions and of differentiating between what is almost extinct and finally extinct. Nevertheless, several species have been eradicated from islands they previously occupied. The frog *Leptodactylus fallax,* the lizards *Leiocephalus herminieri*, *Ameiva major* and *Mabuya bistriata*, and the snake *Liophis cursor* have all been eradicated from Martinique[45] (although the latter may persist on offshore islets). The snake *Clelia errabunda* has been eradicated from St Lucia while *Liophis ornatus* and *Cnemidophorus vanzoi* have been eradicated from the main island (*Liophis ornatus* may now be extinct on its last foothold, Maria Island). The snakes *Liophis melanotus* and *Pseudoboa neuwiedi* are extinct on Grenada and *Liophis perfuscus* and *I. iguana* are extinct on Barbados[45]. The Guadeloupean *Ameiva cineracea* has been eradicated from the main island and is probably also now extinct on the satellite islets[46]. The Lesser Antillean iguana has been eradicated from 7 of the original 16 islands in its range (Antigua, Barbuda, Grande Terre, St Kitts, Nevis, Marie Galante and Îles des Saintes)[47].

CONSERVATION THREATS

Threats to the survival of reptile and amphibian species in the Lesser Antilles include habitat loss, disturbance, unintentional killing, intentional killing, introduced species and natural disasters. These vary greatly in importance.

◈ Habitat loss

Habitat loss occurs in the Lesser Antilles in coastal areas as a result of development for tourism and agriculture. For example, clearing for agriculture has left little littoral woodland **(90)** in the Lesser Antilles, while on the flat islands, e.g. Marie Galante, little natural

90. A remnant of littoral woodland, Atlantic coast, Dominica

91. Cloud forest habitat from Morne Diablotin, Dominica

vegetation remains even in the hinterland. Considerable damage may be done to the vegetation by feral goats, and even where agriculture has been abandoned, these will prevent regeneration of the natural vegetation. On mountainous islands the montane rain forest and transitional forest have also been reduced by agricultural practices, e.g. for citrus and banana plantations. Rain forest trees that are felled to make way for plantations may be left to rot and relatively little damage has occurred recently due to commercial wood harvesting (which is now prohibited on some islands such as Dominica). The relatively inaccessible cloud forests **(91)** do not appear to be perturbed by agriculture. Overall, agricultural practice appears to be having more impact than tourist development. In specific cases, where very rare species are currently restricted to small xeric satellite islets, e.g. the Maria islands **(77)** off St Lucia, fire (natural or accidental) may be a potentially serious hazard.

Disturbance

Some species, e.g. whistling frogs, anoles and house geckos, are extremely resistant to human disturbance, while others, e.g. marine turtles, are extremely susceptible. Heavy local use of beaches and tourism development may prevent turtles from nesting. Other beach nesters, such as iguanas, may also be readily disturbed.

Unintentional killing

Herbicides and pesticides as well as pollution may kill amphibians and reptiles as well as destroying their food or habitat. Discarded plastic bags floating in the sea may be mistaken for jellyfish by turtles, with generally fatal results. Some species, e.g. boas, seem to be frequent casualties of road kills and other species may be vulnerable at particular times, e.g. female iguanas crossing coastal roads to find nesting sites. It is difficult to assess the impact of road kills or agricultural chemicals in the Lesser Antilles. It does not appear to be a major threat but may be locally important at particular times.

Intentional killing

This occurs for food, saleable products and 'pest' control, and also for no particularly good reason. Species that are harvested for food include green (and other) turtles, turtle eggs, iguanas and their eggs, and mountain chickens (*Leptodactylus* frogs). Some of these animals are used for local consumption, but are not a significant protein source. However, harvesting may have damaged some island populations and is implicated as a factor in eradicating iguanas and mountain chickens from particular islands. Currently, there is a specialised market for tourists who want to sample exotic local specialities such as mountain chicken. Until one can be sure of the sustainability of this it should be discouraged. Attempts have been made at iguana ranching outside the Lesser Antilles, but frog farming has to contend with slow development and, at the moment, neither frog nor iguana farming appears realistic, or necessary. The killing of hawksbill turtles for 'tortoise shell' is generally illegal throughout the Lesser Antilles and tourists should avoid purchasing tortoiseshell products, or eating turtle meat.

While any amphibian or reptile may be casually killed without good reason, snakes are particularly subject to this even when they are harmless. In the past, bounties were paid for dead *Bothrops* but in fact venomous snakes pose little threat to humans in the Lesser Antilles as a whole, as they are only found on two of the islands. More needs to be done in educating the public in order to protect individual snake species from this threat.

Introduced species

These may have had a devastating effect in the Lesser Antilles. Introduced animals may prey on, or compete with, naturally occurring species. More insidiously, they may hybridise with them and irreversibly compromise the purity of their gene pool. Some species, e.g. rats, some anoles and whistling frogs, were accidentally introduced, but others, such as man's pets, e.g. cats and dogs, or agricultural animals, e.g. goats and perhaps some iguanas, were deliberately introduced. However, those animals that were introduced for biological pest control (in particular the mongoose, but the marine toad has also been introduced) have perhaps done the greatest damage.

Marine toads may prey on small amphibians and reptiles or poison larger ones that try and eat them. Marine toads have been introduced into several regions of the world as a biological control for sugarcane beetle. This has caused intense conservation problems in some areas (e.g. Australia), without even serving its original purpose as an effective biological control. They are found on numerous islands in the Lesser Antilles, but there is little evidence that they have had as much effect on the local fauna as in Australia.

On the other hand, the other deliberate introduction, the mongoose, may have had a major effect. Originally introduced to kill pit vipers (*Bothrops*) and rodents, they have spread to numerous islands. While they have had little effect on *Bothrops* populations (indeed a large *Bothrops* would regard a mongoose as a suitable prey item), they may have reduced or eradicated numerous terrestrial lizards (notably ground lizards) and colubrid snakes. It is impossible to know whether the mongoose, or another anthropogenic factor, is responsible for the decline of diurnal, ground-dwelling, lowland snakes and lizards. The correlation between the absence of mongoose and the presence of ground-dwelling squamates is not absolute for lizards, but is very close in colubrid snakes. Other anthropogenic factors, such as deliberate killing of snakes or the effects of rats, may have had an impact. However, harmless snakes are killed assiduously on all islands (and despite considerable effort, the mongoose did not succeed in eradicating *Bothrops*) and rats can occur in large numbers on islands with a healthy herpetofauna (e.g. Dominica). The fact remains that no island with mongoose also has large populations of diurnal ground-dwelling lizards and colubrids. Consequently, while further investigation is worth while, the *prima facie* case for the mongoose contributing to the decline of this section of the herpetofauna is very strong. The mongoose may have contributed to the eradication of the Antiguan racer on the main island and its restriction to the mongoose-free islet of Great Bird Island. Similarly, the mongoose may have contributed to the eradication of the St Lucian snake *Liophis ornatus* and lizard *Cnemidophorus vanzoi* on the main island and its restriction to the mongoose-free islet of the Maria Islands.

Other deliberate introductions include goats, cats and dogs. Goats have a significant effect in destroying vegetation in small xeric islands, e.g. satellite islets of Anguilla and St Barts, which, among other effects, may reduce or exclude iguanas. Cats and dogs may not be generally critical. However, they may be instrumental in damaging iguana populations, e.g. feral cats prey on juveniles of the endangered iguana in Anguilla. Common iguanas themselves may have been deliberately spread between islands to provide a food source. Where both common and Lesser Antillean iguanas occur together, the former may replace the latter or pollute the gene pool by hybridisation (as has occurred in Îles des Saintes).

Accidentally introduced rats are widespread in the Lesser Antilles, as they are in the rest of the world. In particular circumstances they can be critically important. For example, on Great Bird Island (a satellite islet of Antigua), they were a key factor threatening the continued existence of one of the world's rarest snakes, as they eat eggs and small snakes[48].

The whistling frog *E. johnstonei* has been widely introduced within the Lesser Antilles beyond its presumed natural range, e.g. into Anguilla[29] and the Grenadines[49] and may represent a serious conservation threat to the other whistling frogs by competitive replacement[50]. Although it may out-compete naturally occurring species (in Guadeloupe and perhaps Martinique) there is evidence to suggest that in many cases it is limited to disturbed habitats and is not replacing the local species from undisturbed habitat, e.g. in Grenada and St Vincent[50]. Nevertheless, ongoing habitat disturbance may facilitate the spread of this frog at the expense of local species. No evidence exists on whether hybridisation between species poses a problem.

However, not all accidental introductions pose a serious problem. For example, the anoles *A. extremus* (from Barbados) and *A. wattsi* (from Antigua) introduced into St Lucia do not appear to be hybridising with the naturally occurring species (*A. luciae*)[51] or spreading rapidly. Nevertheless, competitive replacement remains a potential problem in this situation and vigilance is required.

Natural disasters

The Lesser Antilles are subject to two natural catastrophic processes: hurricanes and volcanic eruption. Hurricanes can do a great deal of damage that takes a long time in human terms to recover. While these are naturally occurring and the ecosystems must have evolved in their presence, they may prove to be the final deciding factor once other factors have produced a critical situation. For example a hurricane may swamp a satellite islet to which a species has been limited, e.g. by mongoose introduction on to the main island, and thus destroy the last remaining individuals of a species. Volcanic eruptions have occurred throughout the geological history of the Lesser Antilles with some massive eruptions in the geologically recent past. For example, a massive eruption (5 times as violent as the famous Krakatau eruption in the 1800s) occurred in Dominica *c.* 30 000 years ago, with the resulting ash deposited on the sea floor up to 240 km to the east, and pyroclastic flows extending 300 km to the south[52]. Currently, the eruption of the Montserrat volcano is endangering components of its fauna, as large areas of rain forest have been damaged[53].

CONSERVATION MEASURES

Many of the causes of the conservation problems are not realistically reversible. One of the main causes of decline is introduced species but it is unlikely that one could eradicate the mongoose or others. Specific conservation measures include habitat protection, rat eradication from specific areas, captive breeding, translocation and education.

Habitat protection is obviously of central importance, particularly where species have very restricted ranges, e.g. the Maria Islands of St Lucia for *Cnemidophorus vanzoi* and *Liophis ornatus*. Other sites that have been established specifically to protect reptiles include Îles de la Petite Terre in Guadeloupe, and the Boven National Park in St Eustatius (primarily for *Iguana delicatissima*). Many islands have protected areas in which endemic reptiles occur even though they were not planned as reptile reserves, e.g. the Morne Trois Piton National Park in Dominica, the National Park in Basse Terre, Guadeloupe, and the Grand Étang Forest Reserve in Grenada.

Rat eradication has been achieved on the satellite islet of Great Bird Island to protect the sole remaining population of the Antiguan racer. This admirable achievement is likely to require constant vigilance to sustain it, as rats are masters at colonisation, and are likely to be assisted by the regular day-trip boat traffic to the island.

Captive breeding may be useful as a last ditch attempt at conservation, offering insurance against chance elimination of small single populations such as the Antiguan racer. Zoos, such as those in Jersey in the Channel Islands and Dallas, Texas, have a sustained reputation in this area. Such captive-bred populations may offer other zoos, which are not able to undertake captive breeding programmes themselves, an opportunity to obtain otherwise unobtainable rare species. Captive breeding programmes are in operation, or under consideration, for the Montserrat mountain chicken, Antiguan racer, Lesser Antillean iguana, and St Lucian whiptail. The ultimate aim of most such programmes is to produce a sufficient number of individuals for seeding new populations in suitable locations. Translocation can also be carried out from the source population directly. However, it can be a difficult task to ensure that proposed translocation sites are suitable in terms of the species' ecological requirements and absence of threats. An example of this is the translocation of the lizard *Cnemidophorus vanzoi* from Maria Major islet to another satellite islet of St Lucia. Similar plans are being considered for the Antiguan racer, using captive-bred specimens to seed a new population.

Finally, education is an essential component of conservation. This may be general or focused on a particular species such as St Lucia's poster campaign on the *Boa constrictor*.

Checklist of Species by Island

Species	Grn	Grnd	StV	Bbds	StL	Mart	Dom	MG	Des	Snts	Guad	Mont	Red	Ant	Bbda	Nev	StK	StE	Saba	StB	StM	Som	Ang
Amphibians																							
Bufo marinus	—		—	—	—	—						—	—	—		—	—				—	—	—
Colostethus chalcopis						×																	
Eleutherodactylus amplinympha							×																
E. barlagnei											×												
E. euphronides	×																						
E. johnstonei	×	—	×	×	×	×	—	—			—	×				×	×	×	×	?	×	×	×
E. martinicensis						×	×	×	×	×	×												
E. pinchoni											×												
E. shrevei			×																				
Leptodactylus fallax						E	×					×											
L. validus	×	×	×																				
Scinax rubra	×																					—	

117

Checklist of Species by Island (continued)

Species	Som	Ang	StM	StB	Saba	StE	StK	Nev	Bbda	Antt	Red	Mont	Guad	Snts	Des	MG	Dom	Mart	StL	Bbds	StV	Grndn	Green
Turtles, tortoises and terrapins																							
Caretta caretta	X	X	X	X	X	X	X	X	X	X	X	X	X	X	X	X	X	X	X	X	X	X	X
Chelonia mydas	X	X	X	X	X	X	X	X	X	X	X	X	X	X	X	X	X	X	X	X	X	X	X
Dermochelys coriacea	X	X	X	X	X	X	X	X	X	X	X	X	X	X	X	X	X	X	X	X	X	X	X
Eretmochelys imbricata	X	X	X	X	X	X	?	X	X	X	X	X	X	X	X	X	X	X	X	X	X	X	X
Geochelone carbonaria		X	X	X		X			X	P	X	X	—				—			—		—	—
Pelusios subniger												X											
Trachemys scripta													—										
T. stejnegeri																—							
Lizards																							
Ameiva ameiva																					P	X	X
A. atrata											E												
A. cineracea													X										
A. corax		X																					

Species	GGreen	GGrndn	StV	BBds	StL	Mart	Dom	MG	Des	Snts	Guad	Mont	Red	Ant	Bbda	Nev	StK	StE	Ssba	StB	StM	Ang	Som
Ameiva corvina																							X
A. erythrocephala																X	X	X					
A. fuscata							X																
A. griswoldi (ground lizard)														X	X								
A. major						E																	
A. pluvianotata												X											
A. plei																				X	X	X	
Anolis aereus	X	X																					
A. bimaculatus																X	X	X					
A. extremus				X	—																		
A. ferreus								X															
A. forresti															X								
A. gingivinus																				X	X	X	X
A. griseus			X																				
A. leachi														X	X								
A. lividus												X											
A. luciae					X																		

Checklist of Species by Island (continued)

Species	Som	Ang	StM	StB	Saba	StE	StK	Nev	Bbda	Ant	Red	Mont	Guad	Snts	Des	MG	Dom	Mart	StL	Bbds	StV	Grnd	Gren
Anolis marmoratus													X	X	X								
A. nubilis											X												
A. oculatus																	X						
A. pogus			X																				
A. richardii																						X	X
A. roquet																		X					
A. sabanus					X																		
A. schwartzi						X	X	X															
A. trinitatis																					X		
A. wattsi										X									—				
Bachia heteropa																						X	X
Cnemidophorus vanzoi																			X				
Diploglossus montisserrati												X											
Gymnophthalmus pleei									X				X				X	X	X				
G. underwoodi													X				?			X	X	X	

Species	Gren	Grnd	StV	Bbds	StL	Mart	Dom	MG	Des	Snts	Guad	Mont	Red	Ant	Bbda	Nev	StK	StE	Saba	StB	StM	Ang	Som
Hemidactylus mabouia	—	—	—	—	—	—	—			—	—	—		—			—	—	—		—	—	×
H. palaich*hus					×	×	×		×	E	×	×		E	E	E	E				×		
Iguana delicatissima										×	×							×		×	×	×	
I. iguana	×	×	×	×	×																		
Kentropyx borckiana																							
Leiocepha.us herminieri						E		E															
Mabuya bistriata	P	×	P	P	P	P	×	×	×	×	×	×	×									×	
Phyllodactylus pulcher				P																			
Sphaerodcctylus elegantulus														×	×								
S. fantasticus							×	×	×	×	×	×											
S. kirbyi		×																					
S. macrolepis																							
S. microlepis					×																		
S. sabanus																×	×	×	×				
S. sputatcr																×	×	×	×	×	×	×	
S. vincenti			×		×	×	×																
Thecadacīylus rapicauda	×	×	×		×	×	×			×	×	×		×	×	×	×	×	×	×	×	×	×

Checklist of Species by Island (continued)

Species	Ang	StMB	Saba	StE	StK	Nev	Bda	Ant	Red	Mont	Guad	Snts	Des	MG	Dom	Mart	StL	Bds	StV	Grnd	Gren
Snakes																					
Alsophis antiguae								×													
A. antillensis										×	×	×	?	×	×						
A. rijersmai	×	×																			
A. rufiventris				×	×	×															
Boa constrictor															×		×				
Bothrops caribbaea																	×				
B. lanceolata																×					
Chironius vincenti																			×		
Clelia clelia																				×	×
C. errabunda																	E				
Corallus hortulanus											?								×	×	×
Leptotyphlops bilineata																×	×		×		
L. tenella																		×			
Liophis cursor																E					

Species	Som	Ang	St M	St B	Saba	St E	St K	Nev	Bbda	Ant	Red	Mont	Guad	Snts	Des	MG	Dom	Mart	St L	Bbds	St V	Gmdn	Gren
Liophis juliae													x	x	?		x						
L. melanotus																						x	P
L. ornatus																			x				
L. perfuscus																				E			
Mastigodryas bruesi																				E	x	x	
Pseudoboa neuwiedi		x																					P
Ramphotyphlops braminus													x										
Typhlops dominicana								x									x						
T. monastus							x	x				x					x						
T. tasymicris																							x
Crocodiles and caimans																							
Caiman crocodilus																						V	V
Crocodylus intermedius																							E

Key to symbols: x = present, E = extinct, I = introduced, V = vagrant, ? = presence unconfirmed, P = probably extinct.
Key to islands: Som = Sombrero, Ang = Anguilla, St M = St Martin, St B = St Barts, Saba = Saba, St E = St Eustatius, St K = St Kitts, Nev = Nevis, Bbda = Barbuda, Ant = Antigua, Red = Redonda, Mont = Montserrat, Guad = Basse Terre and Grande Terre, Snts = Îles des Saintes, Des = Désirade, MG = Marie Galante, Dom = Dominica, Mart = Martinique, St L = St Lucia, Bbds = Barbados, St V = St Vincent, Gmdn = The Grenadines, Gren = Grenada.

Glossary

Adult Sufficiently grown to be sexually mature.

Advanced Of recent evolutionary origin.

Amphibian Able to live both on land and in water.

Amplexus Mating embrace of frogs and toads.

Anterior Front. Towards the head end.

Anuran Jumping amphibian; frog or toad.

Apodan Legless amphibian; caecilean.

Aposematic coloration Bright coloration to warn off a predator.

Aquatic Living in water.

Arboreal Living in trees.

Autotomy When a part of the body (i.e. tail of a lizard) is shed in defence when grasped by an attacker. The tail is usually re-grown.

Axillary Armpit.

Bask Exposing the body to the sun in order to warm up.

Caecilian *See* Apodan.

Carapace The dorsal (top) part of the shell of chelonids (turtles, tortoises and terrapins). *See* Plastron.

Carnivorous Flesh eating.

Cloaca Chamber which receives excreta and reproductive products (e.g. eggs) before passing them through the vent.

Cloud forest High altitude forest in the cloud layer.

Clutch Eggs laid by a female in a single breeding attempt.

Cold-blooded Outdated and incorrect term for an animal whose body temperature varies with that of the environment.

Colonise To establish a breeding population in a new area.

Constriction Coils of a snake squeeze the prey preventing breathing and so causing death.

Crepuscular Active at dawn and dusk.

Crest Raised structure along the mid-dorsal surface of the head, body or tail.

Crural Thighs.

Crypsis Attempting to be hidden or camouflaged.

Dimorphism Two types, as in sexual dimorphism when males and females differ morphologically.

Display A stereotyped behaviour between animals, often associated with mating or defence of territory.

Diurnal Active in the daytime.

Dorsal Upper or topside.

Dorsolateral The upper part of the side of an animal.

Ectotherm An animal that obtains its body heat from external sources (*see* Heliothermic) rather than metabolism.

Endemic Restricted to a specific geographic area.

Family A term used in taxonomy to indicate a level of relationship above that of genus but below that of order.

Fauna Animal species existing at a given time/place.

Femoral pores Pores, in a row, on the underside of the thigh of some lizards. Generally more pronounced in adult males.

Fossorial Burrowing.

Genus (plural: genera) A term used in taxonomy to indicate a group of one or more species that are closely related to one another.

Heliothermic Obtaining warmth from the sun.

Herbivorous Plant eating.

Insectivorous Insect eating.

Interocular Between the eyes.

Iris Coloured ring in the eye surrounding the pupil.

Juvenile Sexually immature young.

Keel Ridge, e.g. on a scale of a snake or carapace of a turtle.

Labial Lip.

Lamellae Bands of bristles (*see* Setae) on the underside of the toes of geckos and anoles.

Larva Immature stage of amphibian (tadpole) before metamorphosis to adult. Typically associated with fresh water or damp conditions.

Lateral Side.

Marine Living in the sea.

Metamorphosis Rapid transformation from a larva to adult (e.g. as in amphibians).

Neotropics Tropical area of the new world (Americas).

Nocturnal Active at night.

Nuchal Neck.

Nuptial pad Rough dark skin on the hands of male amphibians to help grip in amplexus.

Ocellus (plural: ocelli) Coloured spot, often with a contrasting edge.

Omnivorous Eating a range of food from both plants and animals.

Orbital In the region of the eye.

Order A term used in taxonomy to indicate a level of relationship above that of family but below that of class.

Oviparous Egg laying.

Pan-tropical Distributed throughout the tropics.

Parietal Paired bone or region in the roof of the skull.

Parotoid gland Swollen gland behind the eye of amphibians.

Parthenogenesis Asexual reproduction. Parthenogenetic species have no males.

Pectoral girdle Skeleton supporting the forelimb. Pectoral area is the shoulder area.

Pelvic girdle Skeleton supporting the hindlimbs. Pelvic region is where the hindlimbs join the trunk.

Pits Paired heat-sensitive organ on the face of pit vipers between the eye and nostril.

Plastron The ventral (underside) part of the shell of chelonids (turtles, tortoises and terrapins). *See* Carapace.

Posterior Rear. Towards the hind end.

Primitive Of ancient evolutionary origin.

Reticulated Net-like.

Scale In reptiles a flattened plate in the epidermis of the skin.

Scapular Shoulder region.

Scavenging Feeding on dead animals (or plants).

Scute Enlarged scale.

Semiaquatic Living part of the time in water.

Setae Bristles arranged in bands on the underside of the toes of geckos and anoles (assist in climbing on smooth surfaces).

Subtympanic Below the eardrum.

Tadpole The larva of an amphibian.

Temporal An area (the temple) of the skull.

Terrestrial Living on the land.

Tympanum Eardrum.

Unisexual *See* Parthenogenesis.

Urodele Newts and salamanders.

Vent External slit leading to cloaca.

Ventral Lower or underside.

Vertebral stripe Stripe along the mid-dorsal surface.

Viviparous Giving birth to live young.

Vocal sac Inflatable bag-like structure leading from the mouth cavity (e.g. under the throat) of frogs and toads for the resonance of sound.

Web Thin skin between the toes of amphibians.

Xeric Dry (relating to habitat).

References

1. Sigurdsson, H. and S. Carey (1990). *Caribbean Volcanoes: A Field Guide*. Geological Association of Canada, Mineralogical Association of Canada, Society of Economic Geologists, Joint Annual Meeting, Toronto 1991, Field Trip B1: Guidebook, 101pp.
2. Schwartz, A. and R.W. Henderson (1991). *Amphibians and Reptiles of the West Indies: Descriptions, Distributions and Natural History*. University of Florida Press, Gainesville, USA.
3. Kaiser, H., T.F. Sharbel, and D.M. Green (1994). Systematics and biogeography of eastern Caribbean *Eleutherodactylus* (Anura: Leptodactylidae): evidence from allozymes. *Amphibia–Reptilia* **15**: 375–94.
4. Kaiser, H., L.A. Coloma and H.M. Gray (1994). A new species of *Colostethus* (Anura: Dendrobatidae) from Martinique, French Antilles. *Herpetologica* **50**: 23–32.
5. Pritchard, P.C.H. (1979). *Encyclopaedia of Turtles*. TFH publications, New Jersey, USA.
6. Murphy, J.C. (1997). *Amphibians and Reptiles of Trinidad and Tobago*. Krieger Publishing Company, Florida, USA.
7. Campbell, J.A. and W.W. Lamar (1989). *The Venomous Reptiles of Latin America*. Cornell University Press, Ithaca, New York.
8. Bullock D.J. and P.G.H. Evans (1990). The distribution, density and biomass of terrestrial reptiles in Dominica, West Indies. *J. Zool. Lond.* **222**: 421–43.
9. Thorpe, R.S. and A. Malhotra (1996). Molecular and morphological evolution within islands. *Phil. Trans. R. Soc. Lond., Series B Biol. Sci.* **351**:815–22.
10. James, A.A. (1986). *Cabrits Plants and Their Uses*. Forestry & Wildlife Division, Ministry of Agriculture, Commonwealth of Dominica.
11. Carrington, S. (1998). *Wild Plants of the Eastern Caribbean*. Macmillan Education, Basingstoke, UK.
12. Malhotra, A. and R.S. Thorpe (1995). *Ameiva fuscata. Cat. Amer. Amph. Rept.* **606**: 1–3.

13. Evans, P.G.H. (1990). *Birds of the Eastern Caribbean*. Macmillan Education, Basingstoke, UK.

14. Bullock D.J., H.M. Jury and P.G.H. Evans (1993). Foraging ecology in the lizard *Anolis oculatus* (Iguanidae) from Dominica, West Indies. *J. Zool. Lond.* **230**: 19–30.

15. Kaiser, H. and J.D. Hardy Jr (1994). *Eleutherodactylus martinicensis. Cat. Amer. Amph. Rept.* **582**: 1–4.

16. Kaiser, H., D.M. Green and M. Schmid (1994). Systematics and biogeography of Eastern Caribbean frogs (Leptodactylidae: *Eleutherodactylus*), with the description of a new species from Dominica. *Can. J. Zool.* **72**: 2217–37.

17. Kaiser, H. Personal communication.

18. Kaiser, H. (1992). The trade-mediated introduction of *Eleutherodactylus martinicensis* (Anura: Leptodactylidae) on St Barth, French Antilles, and its implication for Lesser Antillean biogeography. *J. Herpetol.* **26**: 264–73.

19. King, F.W. (1962). Systematics of Lesser Antillean lizards of the genus *Sphaerodactylus. Bull. Florida State Mus. Biol. Sci.* **7**(1): 1–52.

20. Kaiser, H. (1994). *Leptodactylus fallax. Cat. Amer. Amph. Rept.* **583**: 1–3.

21. Brooks, G.R. Jr (1982). An analysis of prey consumed by the anuran, *Leptodactylus fallax*, from Dominica, West Indies. *Biotropica* **14**: 301–9.

22. Lescure, J. (1979). Étude taxonomique et eco-ethologique d'un amphibien des Petites Antilles: *Leptodactylus fallax* Muller, 1926 (Leptodactylidae). *Bull. Mus. Natl. Hist. Nat.*, Paris, 4e ser., 1, sect. A (3): 757–74.

23. Underwood, G. (1993). A new snake from St Lucia, West Indies. *Bull. Nat. Hist. Mus. (Zool.)* **59**: 1–9.

24. Underwood, G. Personal communication.

25. Kaiser, H. and R. Wagenseil (1995). Colonisation and distribution of *Eleutherodactylus johnstonei* Barbour (Anura: Leptodactylidae) on Dominica, West Indies. *Carib. J. Sci.* **31**: 341–4.

26. Kaiser, H. and J.D. Hardy Jr (1994). *Eleutherodactylus johnstonei. Cat. Amer. Amph. Rept.* **581**: 1–5.

27. Brooks, G.R. (1983). *Gymnophthalmus pleei* Bocourt: an addition to the lizard fauna of Dominica, West Indies. *Herp. Review* **14**(1): 32.

28. Censky, E.J. and D.R. Paulson (1992). Revision of the *Ameiva* (Reptilia: Teiidae) of the Anguilla Bank, West Indies. *Annals Carnegie Museum* **61**: 177–95.

29. Censky, E.J. (1989). *Eleutherodactylus johnstonei* (Salientia: Leptodactylidae) from Anguilla, West Indies. *Carib. J. Sci.* **25**: 229–31.
30. Daltry, J.C. Personal communication.
31. Roughgarden, J. (1995). *Anolis Lizards of the Caribbean*. Oxford University Press.
32. McLaughlin, J.F. and J. Roughgarden (1989). Avian predation on *Anolis* lizards in the northeastern Caribbean: an inter-island contrast. *Ecology* **70**: 617–28.
33. Duellman, W.E. (1978). The biology of an equatorial herpetofauna in Amazonian Ecuador. *Misc. Publ. Mus. Nat. Hist. Univ. Kansas* **65**: 1–352.
34. McLean, R. (1998). *Saban Trails*. Saba Conservation Foundation, Saba, Netherlands Antilles.
35. Easteal, S. (1986). *Bufo marinus. Cat. Amer. Amph. Rept.* **395**: 1–4.
36. Censky, E.J. and K. Lindsay (1997). *Gymnophthalmus underwoodi*. Lesser Antilles: Barbuda. *Herp.Review* **28**: 210.
37. Jones, A.G., A. Malhotra and R.S. Thorpe. Unpublished data.
38. Reardon, J. Personal communication.
39. Giannasi, N. (1997). Morphological, molecular and behavioural evolution of the *Anolis roquet* group. PhD thesis, University of Wales Bangor.
40. Anthony, D. Personal communication.
41. Carrington, S. (1993). *Wild Plants of Barbados*. Macmillan Press, Basingstoke, UK.
42. Kaiser, H., J.D. Hardy and D.M. Green (1994). Taxonomic status of Caribbean and South American frogs currently ascribed to *Eleutherodactylus urichi* (Anura: Leptodactylidae*). Copeia* (3): 780–96.
43. Lazell, J.D. Jr and T. Sinclair (1990). Geographic distribution: *Gymnophthalmus underwoodi. Herp. Review* **21**(4): 96.
44. Lazell, J.D. Jr (1994). A new *Sphaerodactylus* (Sauria: Gekkonidae) from Bequia, Grenada Bank, Lesser Antilles. *Breviora* **496**: 1–20.
45. Cork, D. (1992). The status and conservation needs of the terrestrial herpetofauna of the Windward Islands (West Indies). *Biol. Conserv.* **62**: 47–58.
46. Baskin, J.N. and E.E. Williams (1996). The Lesser Antillean *Ameiva* (Saria: Teiidae). Re-evaluation, zoogeography and the effects of predation. *Studies on the Fauna of Curaçao and other Caribbean Islands*, **23**: 144–76.

47. Anon. (1998). Lesser Antillean iguana conservation. *Flora and Fauna News* **9**: 4.
48. Anon. (1995). Antigua racer conservation project: Phase 1 preliminary report. *Flora and Fauna Int.,* Cambridge, UK.
49. Henderson, R.W., J. Daudin, G.T. Hass and T.J. McCarthy (1992). Significant distribution records for some amphibians and reptiles in the Lesser Antilles. *Carib. J. Sci.* **28**: 101–3.
50. Kaiser, H. and R.W. Henderson (1994). The conservation status of Lesser Antillean frogs. *Herpetolog. Nat. Hist.* **2**: 41–56.
51. Giannasi, N.C., R.S. Thorpe and A. Malhotra (1997). Introductions of *Anolis* species to the island of St Lucia, West Indies: Testing for hybrids using multivariate morphometrics. *J. Herpetol.* **31**: 586–9.
52. Sigurdsson, H. and S. Carey (1981). Marine tephrochronology and Quaternary explosive volcanism in the Lesser Antilles arc. In R.S.J. Sparks and S. Self (eds), *Tephra Studies*. NATO series, Reidel, Holland, pp. 255–80.
53. Hartley, J. (1998). Rescue plan for Caribbean wildlife. *Oryx* **32**: 104.

Index

Italicised numbers refer to *pages* on which illustrations occur.